THE
YIN AND YANG
OF
AMERICAN CULTURE

Eun Kim is available as a cross-cultural communication consultant/ trainer or speaker.
She can be reached at
e-mail: ceointl@aol.com
phone: 512–343–0472
fax: 512–343–8475

THE YIN AND YANG OF

OF

AMERICAN CULTURE

A PARADOX

EUN Y. KIM

INTERCULTURAL PRESS, INC.

First published by Intercultural Press. For information contact:

Intercultural Press	Nicholas Brealey Publishing
PO Box 700	36 John Street
Yarmouth, Maine 04096 USA	London, WC1N 2AT, UK
001-207-846-5168	44-207-404-0224
Fax: 001-207-846-5181	Fax: 44-207-404-8311
www.interculturalpress.com	www.nbrealey-books.com

Book and cover design and production: Patty J. Topel

Printed in the United States of America

05   04   03   02   01   1   2   3   4   5

Library of Congress Cataloging-in-Publication Data
Kim, Eun Y.
    The yin and yang of American culture: a paradox/Eun Y. Kim.
        p. cm.
Includes bibliographic references.
    ISBN 1-877864-85-4
    1. United States—Civilization—1945–. 2. National characteristics, American. 3. Social values—United States. 4. United States—foreign public opinion, Asian. 5. Public opinion—Asia. I. Title.
E169.12.K464   2001
973.92—dc21   2001024489

Dedication

Dedicated to my son, Lincoln Gates Valdez, and his generation that will seek to understand their own culture and other cultures as citizens of the world and to transform their culture into world class to be respected and saluted by the people all over the world.

Contents

Week 3
Rb 23 - 25

Part Two—The Yin of American Culture: Liberation of American Vices

Part Three—Invitation to Global Virtues

Preface

On Friday, October 13, 2000, when I arrived at the Trinity University Auditorium in San Antonio, Texas, I received an envelope with "A Message from the President of the United States" written on it. Like other people who received identical envelopes, I carefully and respectfully opened it and read the letter inside.

Dear Fellow American:

I want to congratulate you on reaching the impressive milestone of becoming a citizen of our great nation. As you enjoy the benefits of American citizenship and assume the responsibilities that accompany it, you

follow the many brave men and women
who have sacrificed to establish and preserve our democracy over the last two
centuries.

You now share in a great experiment: a
nation dedicated to the ideal that all of us
are created equal, a nation with profound
respect for individual rights.

Sincerely,

Bill Clinton

That day, I was being sworn in as an American citizen, along
with 419 others from fifty-six different countries. While
everyone was sharing and celebrating the joy of becoming
an American, I reflected somberly on my life and how I had
got there.

It has been a long journey from Korea, where I had my
first interactions with Americans when I was only eight
years old. My father, who was an educator, believed in
foreign language education during early childhood and sent
me to a language institute in Seoul when I was a third-
grader. It was a place for American children in Korea to
learn English, but for me it was a place to learn English as
a second language and to experience American people and
culture. All Koreans have had a close acquaintanceship with
America since the Korean War. In school, we studied the
contributions of numerous Americans, including George
Washington, Thomas Edison, Benjamin Franklin, Harry
Truman, John F. Kennedy, and Martin Luther King. We had
to memorize Lincoln's Gettysburg Address, Roosevelt's Four

Freedoms, and the Monroe Doctrine. For fun and play, we saw American movies like *Ben-Hur*, *The Sound of Music*, *Love Story*, *Gone with the Wind*, *Rocky*, and *Saturday Night Fever*. We listened to Elvis Presley; Peter, Paul, and Mary; Carly Simon; Barbra Streisand; and Neil Diamond. We read O'Henry, Edgar Allan Poe, John Steinbeck, Ralph Waldo Emerson, and Henry David Thoreau and recited the poems of Henry Wadsworth Longfellow and Robert Frost. As college students, we discussed issues from *Time* and *Newsweek* and sang "We Shall Overcome" when we demonstrated against our government.

Through these experiences, we grew up with a fascination for America. We looked up to Americans as "superior" people and perceived America as a symbol of all virtues. We admired Americans as intelligent, rational, civil, clean, fair, generous, and sophisticated and envied those who had the opportunity to go to the United States. If someone was said to be Americanized, it was a compliment. Thus, when I came to America as a graduate student in the early 1980s, I embraced my new environment and was ready to adopt the American way. I was eager to experience a "real" American life, despite the fact that I moved to Texas, which, as I later learned, some Americans perceive as a foreign country. Knowing that I had a limited time to complete my graduate degrees, I wanted to maximize my experiences in the U.S. I traveled from Hawaii to the Virgin Islands and climbed Mount Rainier and a couple of the Great Smoky Mountains. I visited cities from Boston to Laredo and attended the Indy 500 and many pro football games. I went to as many parties, plays, musicals, and concerts as I could afford. I attended American churches, visited American homes, and simply hung out with Americans. I worked with Americans as a graduate student and joined an American management consulting firm after completing my graduate degrees. Wherever I went, I searched for the good in America and tried to incorporate it into my values. Consciously and unconsciously, I was happy to be Americanized.

When I returned to Korea and traveled to other Asian countries in the 1990s, however, I found that the image of America had changed. People started talking about "ugly Americans." They asked me if I thought America was a nation in decline and described Americans as having little integrity, next to no shame, and no family values. In the eyes of many Asians, Americans were not virtuous anymore; rather, they were selfish, ignorant, ruthless, materialistic, loud, and violent. Consequently, Asian elders feared their young people would be Americanized, and some leaders still warn against the "germs" that Americans might spread to their young people. Despite their concern, American culture has seeped into the lives of most Asians. What is "cool" is often what is from America, especially to the young. The American image sells from Seoul to Bangkok.

Some Asians criticize Americans for their "cultural superiority" or "cultural imperialism." American culture is, unfortunately, often misunderstood in Asia; many Asians form their perceptions of America from media portrayals and short interactions with Americans. Some Asians unknowingly confuse modernization for Westernization or Americanization. Values change with industrialization, and as Asian countries become industrialized, Asian values are affected both positively and negatively. Yet some Asians stereotype all negative effects of industrialization as Western or American. It is often said, "If Asians like something, it's 'modern.' If they don't, it's 'Western.'"

At the same time, few would deny that American values are in serious trouble, and many Americans are confused about their cultural identities. Many "hyphenated" Americans claim their own values, and even more Americans demand that their own values be acknowledged. On the one hand, they want to maintain American values, and on the other hand, they are asking, "What are my values?" In the process, Americans are forgetting the great American ideals and principles the country was built on.

The American experience of each individual is different. Given the diverse population and the variations in race, ethnicity, family style, moral value, work experience, religion, political view, and geographic location, it is hard to generalize Americans. In virtually all aspects of American life, people have differences. Nevertheless, there are similar characteristics that all Americans share, regardless of their age, race, gender, or ethnicity: the common denominators of idealism, egalitarianism, legalism, optimism, and other American values. These are manifest in their American dreams, attitudes, beliefs, communication, dress, etiquette, and lifestyle. Non-Americans frequently observe the unique characteristics that set Americans apart from people in other countries. Many are positive characteristics that have built America and will continue to make America great. They are American virtues to be renewed. Yet there are some practices that, if continued, will cause America to decline. They are American vices to be corrected.

American virtues and vices, interestingly, fit well into the Asian philosophy of *yin* and *yang*. The earliest reference to yin and yang in Chinese history dates to about 700 B.C. Since then, these complementary opposites have influenced Asians as they seek harmony and balance in the universe and in their lives, and they have been applied to government, medicine, relationships, and so on. According to the principle of yin and yang, life is governed by the interaction of two opposite poles, the ultimate of male (yang) and female (yin), positive and negative, light and dark, hard and soft, and any other opposing poles you can imagine. Heaven, the sun, and the fire are yang; earth, the moon, and water are yin. It should be noted, however, that yin and yang are not a dualism in the Western context, like that between good and evil. On the contrary, yin and yang forces coexist in everything. Yin and yang complete each other to maintain cosmic harmony and can even transform into each other. For example, winter, which is yin, changes into summer, which is yang. Furthermore, an entity regarded as yin in one light can be regarded as yang in another light. So, in American vices, there is the possibility of virtue; in American virtues, there is the potential for vice. Abraham Lincoln saw this dualism in America and said, "It has been my experience that folks who have no vices have very few virtues."

This book is written for all Americans who desire to understand American culture and transform it. As Lew Platt, former CEO of Hewlett-Packard, said, "It's imperative that we continually seek to know ourselves better as Americans before we presume to understand others; the realities of globalization demand it, business effectiveness requires it, and diversity depends on it." Readers will recognize, reinforce, and renew the virtues that the world admires about America. Only when they know their common strengths will Americans feel secure enough to embrace changes in the world. At the same time, this book provides insights, from an Asian perspective, into the weaknesses of American society and suggests ways to reverse the decline of some aspects of American culture. For more than one hundred years, the United States has influenced the lives of Asians, but it has been a one-way street. It is time for Americans to open their minds and hearts to Asian culture and values, which have existed for thousands of years. Asians have seen things that Americans have not seen. Asia may not be advanced technologically, but it is advanced philosophically. Asia is a place of many civilizations, and Asians have different perceptions of life and alternative ways to reach happiness. Although Asian perspectives do not provide the answers to all the problems confronting America, they can provide Americans with fresh insights into their problems, and the wisdom of Asia can inspire and comfort Americans.

The new generation in America is a global generation, which will work closely with people from different cultures. Tremendous cultural diversity exists in the United States; already, almost one out of nine Americans is foreign born, and many Americans have foreign-born parents or grand-parents. Some even say that America should be called the United Nations of America instead of the United States of America. Domestic diversity, however, is not enough. To continue to be citizens of a great nation, Americans must transform their sense of nationalism into a sense of interna-tionalism. To reach others and understand them, Ameri-cans must open their eyes and their hearts. Asian countries benefited when their leaders opened their eyes to the West and accepted and sometimes adopted what was good there. Likewise, Americans will benefit from recognizing Asian cultural traditions and adopting positive aspects of Asian culture.

Although this book is intended for Americans, I am hopeful that it will also help Asians better understand Americans, so that both can establish a common ground for mutual understanding. By recognizing each other's merits and weaknesses, Americans and Asians can enrich their own cultures. As more interactions occur between Americans and Asians, it is critical for both to look beyond their superficial understanding of each other. Some friends and colleagues have kindly described me as representing the best qualities of East and West, and I am pressing toward that goal. But if I have any resemblance to such a person, it is thanks to my learning, living, and working in America. For the last three decades, I have had opportunities to learn from Americans as a student, friend, neighbor, colleague, consultant, and trainer. Through my marriage to an American, I have deepened my understanding of American families as a wife, mother, and in-law. At the same time, I am who I am because of my Asian upbringing, which valued family, loyalty, modesty, peace, and harmony.

It would be impossible for one writer to learn about, understand, and present the immense diversity of American culture and its people in a fair, clear, and comprehensive manner. It would also be impossible for one Asian to speak for all Asians. I am only one of 3.3 billion Asians with tremendous cultural, ethnic, and religious diversity. Furthermore, my Asian perspective is based more on the

Confucianism, Buddhism, and Taoism of East Asia than on the Muslim and Hindu cultures of South Asia. But this book is not written from only one person's point of view. Countless individuals—Americans and non-Americans—have shared their insights on American and Asian cultural values; also, a number of friends, colleagues, and clients throughout the world have shared their experiences with me. I owe my cross-cultural knowledge and understanding to numerous scholars in the fields of intercultural communication, American culture, and Asian studies, including Edward T. Hall, Philip H. Harris, Geert Hofstede, L. Robert Kohls, Robert Moran, Yutang Lin, Herrlee G. Creel, and Lucian W. Pye.

My husband, Edward Valdez, was an intimate collaborator in the planning, researching, and writing of this book. He was my principal adviser and also a research subject in our cross-cultural laboratory at home. I also thank my father, who foresaw the need for a global mindset and English competency and required his four daughters to attend foreign language institutes and to memorize five English words every day, even though he could speak no English at all.

My deepest gratitude goes to the editors at Intercultural Press, who saw the need for this book. Working with them was sometimes a struggle between my Asian way and their American way: the goal of the West is to seek truth and find an answer; the way of the East is to have a philosophy of life. Thanks to their relentless curiosity, I was forced to think further, and the book has profited immeasurably.

I would like to clarify two things. First, throughout the book, I use the word *Americans* to describe U.S. citizens and

America as an alternative to the *United States,* because much of the world uses these terms similarly. However, I am aware that Canadians, Central Americans, and South Americans also call themselves Americans. I mean no disrespect to these people. Second, my characterization of certain American and Asian behaviors and traits simply indicates a greater frequency of these behaviors among Americans and Asians than among non-Americans and non-Asians. As a cross-cultural practitioner, I try to avoid stereotyping or overgeneralizing a country's culture, because in every country, people exhibit an entire spectrum of cultural dimensions.

I want to thank all the Americans who contributed their insights about America. I also want to thank this great nation that inspires people throughout the world. "What an extraordinary vision America still is to people overseas," said Ted Koppel, a television journalist who was born in Germany and educated in England. I hope America will become an extraordinary vision to Americans themselves as they renew their virtues with a view toward the Global Century.

Introduction

America in the Twenty-First Century

The Hyperpower: Foreign and Self-Perceptions of Americans

According to the August 1999 issue of *National Geographic*, the new global culture is American culture. Many people already use *Westernized* and *Americanized* interchangeably, and soon the world culture is going to resemble American culture. Recognizing the omnipresence of American culture around the globe, the French have coined a new term to describe America—the *hyperpower*. The term *superpower* was inadequate to convey America's authority and influence in the world. In a *Wall Street Journal* article, Alan Murray wrote:

> It is difficult to find another moment in history when a single nation or political

entity so dominated world affairs. The
Roman Empire, for all its glory, was largely
confined to Europe. The nomads of Central
Asia, led by warriors like Genghis Khan,
spread their influence from Eastern Europe
to China in the thirteenth, fourteenth,
fifteenth centuries, but their cultural influence was limited. Even the British Empire,
on which the sun never set, didn't have the
unrivaled position that America enjoys
today.[1]

Indeed, I have experienced the power of American
culture wherever I have gone. *Titanic*, CNN, *Friends*, *Oprah*,
and the Backstreet Boys have followed me to Japan, Korea,
Thailand, Australia, France, and Italy. U.S. entertainment is
the second largest export industry; American films, music,
and books fascinate both young and old around the globe.
Young Singaporeans claim that they speak American English because they watch American films, even though their
country was a British colony. Even the British say that the
American "Hi, there" has been accepted for use in their e-
mail because the United States dominates information technology. Mickey Mouse, Pooh, Elmo, and Barbie are friends
of the children of the world. McDonald's currently operates
in more than one hundred countries: there are more than
two thousand McDonald's restaurants in Japan; in Beijing,
people wait in line for half an hour to get a Big Mac; in
Australia, 5 percent of the population already eats at
McDonald's (compared with 7 percent in the U.S.).

Not everyone, however, is happy about seeing America
around the world; people fear the possibility of one "Big

MacWorld." There is criticism of the "cultural assault" of companies such as McDonald's, Coca-Cola, Disney, and Nike and of American English. "Cultural imperialism is no joke," wrote Jeffrey Garten, dean of the Yale Graduate School of Management. Jack Lang, the former minister of culture of France, cited American culture as "pure entertainment without restraint, without shame." When I attended a lecture on Japanese e-commerce, the speaker said that what he feared most about e-commerce was the Americanization of Japan.

American images sell from Tokyo to Moscow, but they have also instigated locals to criticize American culture through such books as *The China that Can Say No, The Japan that Can Say No, Culture Jam: The Uncooling of America,* and *The Voice of Asia.* Leaders in Canada, France, Egypt, and Iran have warned against the influx of American culture in their countries and have taken measures to counteract it.

Most people in the world admit that they have a love-hate relationship with America. They love the spirit of America, but they resent something about America, either attitude or lifestyle. When I asked more than one thousand non-Americans about the United States, many of them shared both positive and negative feelings about the country and its people. They admire Americans for being

- ambitious
- diverse
- free
- creative
- fun loving
- friendly

- wealthy
- rules oriented
- open
- energetic
- independent
- adventurous

- generous
- competitive

- optimistic
- trusting

At the same time, many hold negative images of Americans, including their tendency to be

- ethnocentric
- materialistic
- promiscuous
- disloyal
- lacking in family values
- loud
- arrogant
- selfish
- indulgent
- insincere

- aggressive
- inflexible
- impersonal
- superficial
- violent
- youth oriented
- lonely
- spoiled
- lazy
- prejudiced

But do Americans care about how others see them? Should they? Over the years, I have asked more than fifteen hundred American participants in my seminars about their perceptions of Americans, and I found that Americans love being American and are proud of their country. Almost all believe that America is the most powerful nation in the world with the best government, technology, medical facilities, standard of living, higher education, and military power. They are proud of living in a land of opportunity and enjoy their freedoms—from freedom of speech to free spiritedness. They believe in looking out for number one, which, they think, makes them creative, innovative, intelligent, and successful. They admire other Americans' risk-taking and entrepreneurial spirit. They understand that they have a huge impact on the world market and world peace, and some even believe that America should be a model for democracy and human rights. Americans perceive themselves as being extremely sports and leisure oriented because they pursue fun in life. Yet most of them also believe that Americans are hardworking and value time and progress. As "tough guys," they see themselves as persistent, as never giving up; yet they think that they are open, friendly, and hospitable. And they take pride in women's achievements.

Of course, some Americans are not so eager to praise their own country and fellow citizens. Although they are a minority, they share the negative images of Americans held by non-Americans. They criticize their country for too much emphasis on money, image, glamour, and youth. They think that the public education system has failed its citizens, causing incompetence in math and science. They are concerned that Americans do not respect the institution of marriage or their elders. Finally, they fear that the American government is interfering in other countries' affairs.

negatives

Interestingly, when I ask Americans how they think foreigners perceive Americans, even those with positive perceptions of themselves turn negative. Despite their pride in their country and people, the majority believe that the image of the "ugly American" is prevalent overseas. They admit that they are ashamed of the ugly Americans they have seen or met overseas.

Nevertheless, when they discuss the American image abroad, I do not sense that they are genuinely concerned about how they are perceived. In fact, they seem to have fun imagining foreigners bashing Americans. Most of them feel that foreign impressions are shaped by media and Hollywood images, from John Wayne to *Baywatch*. So they feel no need to worry about these images. Although these may be only perceptions, they often reflect reality and can become reality.

Writing about early immigrants, J. Hector St. John de Crèvecoeur wrote, "An American is one who leaves behind him all his ancient prejudices and manners and receives new ones from the new mode of life he has embraced."

Closing of the American Mind

Without doubt, the whole world has embraced some aspects of American culture. Unfortunately, though, Americans have rarely looked to the rest of the world as a source of learning during the last century. Goods have been exchanged and technologies transferred, but the cultural transfer has been mostly one way from America to other countries. During the recession in the 1980s, it was fashionable to cite Japan as a model. American scholars and pundits looked to Japan as a source of inspiration for everything from management practices to manufacturing technology, from education to customer service. But when Japan's economy collapsed and the Asian crisis occurred in the 1990s, America regained its confidence as world leader in everything.

This is a mixed blessing, because pride can close American minds even more tightly. Some Americans already believe that American culture is the universal norm. To them, America is the center of the universe, and foreign behaviors are abnormal. One American tourist had to remind her fellow travelers that foreigners are not defective Americans.

Inside and outside the United States, Americans have been criticized for their ignorance of other cultures. Very few people know the number of European Union (EU) countries, and they are rarely able to name them. Some Americans ask Europeans how they celebrate Thanksgiving. Others ask the British, "How do you celebrate July 4?"

Americans are even less knowledgeable about Asia. In a survey done by the Asia Society in the late 1990s, almost half the respondents did not know that the Pacific Ocean divides the United States and Asia. Some think that Asia is one vast country encompassing Japan, Singapore, China, Korea, and Vietnam. On Jay Leno's *Tonight Show*, an interviewee answered that China had attacked Pearl Harbor. I have met some Americans who can't distinguish the Korean War from the Vietnam War. During the Asian economic crisis in the late 1990s, few Americans, including those who did business with Asia, could name the three countries that had received the International Monetary Fund (IMF) bailout. An American professor of sociology labeled Americans "monolingual, geographically challenged nationalists."

This lack of global literacy is not necessarily the fault of individual Americans. Many high schools do not require world history, geography, or a foreign language. Although American best-sellers are widely translated and read in other countries, rarely do Americans read books written by foreign authors. Even a Nobel Prize winner in literature from another country may find it difficult to find a New York publisher, let alone American readers.

Maybe Americans are losing interest in the outside world as the United States becomes the dominant power. With all the comforts they have, Americans may not feel the need to know about other cultures in their pursuit of liberty and happiness. I can fully understand the feeling. A few years ago, I was traveling through the New England states. As I drove by beautiful, spacious homes in peaceful neighborhoods with luscious green, sculpted lawns, I asked myself why Americans should care about people of other countries—how others live, work, think, and feel—when they have so much where they are. Besides, America is so huge; it could easily be ten different countries. Although I love traveling, it took me almost eighteen years to visit forty states. Sometimes I defend Americans when others complain about their lack of interest in other cultures. I tell them not to blame Americans, because it is not easy for them to learn about other states in their own country, let alone other countries.

Nevertheless, neither the size of the United States nor the complacency of Americans should discourage them from learning about other cultures. More than ever, Americans are connected to the people of other countries—economically, politically, and even environmentally. In 1998 I eagerly rushed home to Austin, Texas, from a business trip to Seoul. The air there had been almost unbearable due to pollution and the sandy winds blown from China's Gobi Desert. I was glad to be on the plane, expecting to breathe relatively clean air in Austin. But when I got there, I found that the air was no better than in Seoul. Smoke from a big fire in Mexico had blown into Texas, and there were health warnings regarding outdoor activities for the elderly and those with respiratory problems. No one country can solve the world's ecological, economic, environmental, and political problems. With all the power it has,

America needs to work with other countries to make the world a more livable and peaceful place.

Opening of the American Mind

As a country of immigrants, America has always been open to other cultures. Americans have reinvented pizza and adopted many other ethnic foods. They are eating more salsa than ketchup and drinking cappuccino and espresso even in small towns. Americans are listening to Latin music in Spanish, applying henna paste, and taking martial arts for mental and physical discipline. But the fact that someone eats sushi with chopsticks, uses alternative medicine, or shops at Pier 1 Imports may have nothing to do with his or her being worldly or open-minded. Despite the phenomenal success of Japanese cars, Walkman, Nintendo, and Pokemon, most Americans do not know the essence of Japanese culture, much less the cultures of lesser-known countries.

If we could shrink the world population to 1,000 people, there would be 584 Asians, 124 Africans, 95 Europeans, 84 Central and South Americans, 55 Russians and others from the former Soviet Union, 52 North Americans, and 6 Australians and New Zealanders. According to Bob Dillenschneider, as quoted by Dr. Robert Schuller of the Crystal Cathedral in Garden Grove, California, in a global village of 100 people as a microcosm representing all the earth's inhabitants, there would be 70 nonwhites and 30 whites; 67 non-Christians and 33 Christians. In that village, 80 people would live in substandard housing, and 50 people would suffer from malnutrition. Seventy-five people would never have made

Global village stats

a telephone call, and fewer than 10 would have access to the Internet. Half of the wealth of the entire village would be in the hands of 6 people, all of whom would be U.S. citizens. When we consider our world from such a global perspective, the need for learning about other cultures becomes apparent. Without an understanding of the cultures of co-workers, customers, partners, and suppliers, America's leadership and dominance are at risk.

If Americans are to be effective in a global village, personally and professionally, they must understand American culture from a cross-cultural perspective. There are many elements of culture, but most of them are outside of our awareness. Culture is like water, and people are like fish. When people are in the water (their own culture), they take it for granted. Only when they find themselves out of the water (their element) do they realize that they need certain "currents," "temperatures," and "minerals" to survive and prosper. As a result, most people who have never traveled outside their home country assume that their values are applied universally. Of course, there are universal values, but depending on its history, geography, religion, economy, politics, and so on, each culture has different beliefs and attitudes, ethics and justice systems, decision-making processes, communication styles, interpersonal relationships, entertainment, food and diet, and the like. Each group is different, and people's unique culture forms their outlook on life, their view of the world, and their beliefs about proper attitudes and behaviors. No one can judge that all is good or all is evil. People develop different ways of thinking and living in order to survive and thrive, depending on their specific circumstances. We cannot say that one is right and the other wrong. Each culture has its own virtues and vices, and every culture has room for improvement.

To experience other cultures, there is no substitute for travel. Chuang Tzu, a Chinese philosopher, said:

> How shall I talk of the sea to the frog if he has never left his pond?
>
> How shall I talk of the frost to the bird of the summer land if it has never left the land of its birth?
>
> How shall I talk of life with the sage, if he is prisoner of his doctrine?

Chap 2 Stp quote

On the road, we come across people we would be unlikely to meet in our own comfort zone. For people who have traveled the world, there is no turning back. Thus, Mark Twain said that travel is fatal to prejudice, bigotry, and narrow-mindedness. Indeed, traveling can be a life-transforming experience.

Although overseas travel definitely broadens one's horizon, Americans do not have to travel to experience other cultures. America is a great place for learning about world cultures. Annually, fifty million international tourists visit the United States, and there is already tremendous cultural diversity among its inhabitants. We can learn a lot about the world when we open our minds and hearts.

Unfortunately, not everyone is ready to embrace global diversity. One superintendent of a Texas school district said that whenever she tried to introduce a multicultural or global curriculum, she faced resistance from board members because they feared that by learning cultural differ-

Fear

ences, the children would lose their American identity. Some people feel threatened by newcomers who look different or speak with accents. A columnist who wrote on multicultural manners in the *Los Angeles Times* said that she often received angry letters from readers. They wrote, "Why should we learn about the cultures of new immigrants? They came to my country, and they have to learn the American way." These people have a point, but their rejection of other cultures only limits their growth and closes the door to a more fulfilling future.

limits growth

The biggest potential benefit of Americans' appreciating other cultures is the transformation of American culture into a world-class culture that can be respected by other nations. The possibilities are limitless if Americans are only willing to accept them.

Vision of a World-Class Culture

"Is America #1?" was the title of a feature on ABC's *20/20* broadcast in 1999. The question may have been a rhetorical one, because there were no criteria for determining number-one status. Ranking countries is a difficult task because there are no established standards for measuring a country's greatness. Per capita gross national product (GNP), standard of living, quality of life, openness of the system, financial success, freedom, and human rights issues have been used to compare nations, but none of them can measure a country's greatness based on its cultural and moral leadership. Nevertheless, there is no doubt that most Americans are convinced that America is one of the greatest countries (if not the greatest) in the world. Very few Americans would give up their U.S. citizenship to live in another country, and almost one million people immigrate to the United States every year.

Although many people think that China poses the biggest challenge to the United States' world-power status in the next one hundred years, most Americans are pretty optimistic (complacent) about America's role as the leader for this century. However, this refutes the historical axiom, "Thirty years prosperity, thirty years decay." It also challenges a Japanese belief that he who climbs a great mountain must come down the other side. The U.S. already climbed a great mountain in the twentieth century. Must it now descend?

Americans are not ready to come down the other side. In a 1999 poll, "The Century Survey," by the *Wall Street Journal* and NBC News, Americans were asked, "Will the United States continue to lead the world?" Most respondents answered yes, and others responded that America will remain strong, even if not a leader. When asked in what specific areas the U.S. ranked as a leader in the last century, 60 percent of the respondents answered movies, music, television, and pop culture; 55 percent, military; 46 percent, technology; 44 percent, world economy; and 44 percent, creativity and innovation (respondents were allowed to pick more than one). Yet when they were asked about the greatest threat to U.S. power status, 74 percent ranked moral decline highest.

Indeed, Americans can boast of great accomplishments: technology (including biotechnology and the Internet), the military, higher education, highways, hospitals, and so on. Even so, the answer to the question whether America is number one may not be a resounding yes. Even if Americans think so, people in other countries might not agree. A writer in a British magazine stated, "I choose to measure America against its own vast, self-satisfied claims. It is not morally superior to the rest of us. It is not the noblest, finest, most decent society that ever was."

Yet as a new American, I have a dream that someday Americans will be respected and admired by people the world over, not because of their economic power but because of their cultural power. I have a vision that someday America will be recognized as the "noblest, finest, most decent society that ever was." These world-class Americans should have in common not only a U.S. passport but also commendable cultural values, ethics, and character.

In one of the documents published by the Immigration and Naturalization Service is the phrase, "those who are privileged to live in the U.S." As a newcomer to the United States and a traveler of the world, I firmly believe that America is a blessed nation and that its residents are privileged to call it home. But the blessings do not come without obligations. The Bible says that those who are given more will be asked to do more. Therefore, old and new Americans alike must ask themselves what more they can do to be worthy of the privileges and prestige they enjoy. Throughout American history, new immigrants have brought their own traditions and combined them with existing American practices. The cultures of the world have come together in this country to weave a rich and intricate tapestry. If all Americans can enrich that tapestry with the finest virtues from all the cultures they represent, they can make it truly world class.

Columnist George Will said, "The culture of the society is more important than the politics of the society in determining its success." It is the job of every American to make his or her culture worthy of respect. A nation's destiny is not in its technology or in the amount of information it acquires—it is in its character. George Santayana wrote, "To be an American is of itself almost a moral condition, an education, and a career." If this is true, and I believe it is, then all Americans have a goal to aspire to: world-class citizenship. To reach this goal, they must earnestly study their present conditions and examine their moral strengths and weaknesses, their cultural assets and liabilities. Being the only remaining superpower is an awesome responsibility for America and its citizens. Whether it is intentional or not, Americans are transferring their values to other nations throughout the world—and some are blindly adopting them. The challenge to Americans is to rediscover what made America great. By celebrating American virtues and liberating American vices, they can transform American culture and make America worthy to lead the world in the twenty-first century.

Part One

The Yang of American Culture: Celebration of American Virtues

This chapter examines what makes America great. There are many things wonderful and right about America. I call them the yang of American culture, because yang represents positive energy, the root of America's power, strength, and commendable characteristics. The original meaning of yang was the sunny side of a hill, whereas yin was the dark side. Yang represents the light, hard, masculine, and upward, whereas yin represents the dark, soft, feminine, and downward. All things in the universe consist of varying proportions of yin and yang.

However, as discussed earlier, yin and yang are not necessarily opposite but are often complementary and interdependent. Each phenomenon can be itself and its opposite. Each phenomenon may be primarily yang or yin but always contains the seed of its opposite within itself. Within yang, there is a potential for yin, and within yin, there is the potential for yang. Yang can change into yin, and vice versa.

Although yang is positive, when taken to the extreme it turns negative and reverts to yin. Thus, positive American characteristics can become negative ones if they are taken to the extreme. For example, the spirit of egalitarianism is commendable, but within it is the seed for entitlement and lack of decorum. Although competition is good, if it is overemphasized, it will make cooperation impossible and create warring tribes. Daring to be oneself is good, but there will be no unity if everyone demands uniqueness. So even in celebrating American virtues, it is important to remember the dualistic nature of yin and yang. I suggest some strategies to prevent virtues from turning into vices, and I encourage readers to do the same, thinking of creative ways to renew American virtues without losing balance.

Dreaming the Impossible

"DREAM IT, BE IT." I saw a young man wearing a T-shirt with that slogan in Anchorage, Alaska. Since the birth of America, this nation has brought together diverse people to realize the power of their dreams. This is the country built by dreamers and by their children. The commonality of their fate is that many chose to come to America to better their lives, with the belief that in this country they could make their dreams come true.

During my last trip to New York, I took a cab. In contrast

with New York cabdrivers' reputation for being notoriously ill-tempered, this particular driver was extremely friendly. He told me that he enjoyed meeting diverse people on his job—from famous television personalities to accidental tourists. As he approached my destination, he showed me an audiotape titled "The Funniest Cabdriver in New York." It was a recording of funny conversations with customers in his cab, and he was selling them for seven dollars each. "Someday, I would like to have my own syndicated radio talk show," he said. I don't know whether he has realized his aspiration, but I think of it as the essence of the American dream. Only in America can people dream big dreams regardless of their background or circumstances.

Most Americans believe in "Be all that you can be." Gulf War hero General Norman Schwarzkopf commented that when the army adopted that slogan, it suddenly started seeing more young soldiers who wanted to make something of their lives. In fact, "Be all that you can be" has become more than a recruitment slogan. It is a way of life for many Americans who seek to overcome barriers to self-fulfillment. Nothing is more distinctive than Americans' disbelief in impossibilities. Every day Americans receive invitations to dream big dreams, and they give the traditional exuberant American answer, "Why not!"

In contrast, many Asians believe that things happen as a result of fate: their success or failure in life, work, and marriage is determined by the year, month, date, hour, and place of their birth. Because they believe that their futures were laid out at birth, many people passively accept undesirable conditions rather than try to shape or alter their destinies. Interestingly, in Chinese, the word for *destiny*

Asian Belief in fate

consists of two characters. The first, *woon,* means "dynamic flow," and the second, *myung,* means "movement of the absolute." Some argue that there is one aspect of life that a person can change, woon, and one that cannot be changed, myung, the larger plan of the universe. However, from birth, Asians are supposed to know who they are and where they fit into their society. In Korea, where I grew up, I was often reminded of an old Korean saying, "Don't even look at a tree if you cannot climb it." We were told that it is a virtue to know one's limitations.

Korean saying

Recently, growing prosperity and democratic ideals have given Asians confidence and opportunities to create their own destinies. Capitalism has provided the means to create one's own fate, and democracy is breaking the chain of vertical relationships and the vicious circle of oppression. Thus, we see Asians dreaming their China dreams in Beijing and their Singapore dreams in Singapore. Nevertheless, a residue of fatalism remains. If a person from an unprivileged class has an ambitious dream, he or she can be condemned as presumptuous. Even when it comes to investment, people often say, "One can't become rich through smart investment. Money must follow him (by predetermination)." Due to this cultural orientation, many Asians still believe that their lot was determined by a divine force before they were born.

Divine force

In contrast, Americans are told, "Know your limits and ignore them." This sky's-the-limit outlook has enabled them to create one of the world's wealthiest nations in a very short time. Leaders such as Benjamin Franklin and Horatio Alger encouraged people to pursue wealth through hard work. Universities use Napoleon Hill's *Think and Grow Rich* as a textbook in classes on American success. Such an atmosphere has produced world-renowned rich people such as Rockefeller, Ford, Du Pont, Carnegie, and Gates. It is not a coincidence that the greatest concentration of wealth is in the United States.

In a London newspaper, John Caline wrote:

> We Europeans correctly like to note that Americans lack irony, which means they lack an adult sense of life's limitations, which means they lack wisdom. But the other side of that coin is that in their adolescent brio they have a sense of possibility, a random energy and optimism that drives them to heights of inventiveness and wealth creation to which we world-weary Europeans would not think to aspire.[2]

This energy inspires and challenges even nonnative citizens to think big. According to *Forbes* magazine, out of the four hundred richest Americans, twenty-two are new immigrants who have realized the power of their dream in the land of "I can."

In addition to dreams of accumulating megawealth, Americans have filled their history with other seemingly impossible dreams. Going to the moon is a great example. I still remember the voice of Neil Armstrong when he first landed on the moon. Even after thirty years, I am awed by this audacious dream. Other achievements are also testimony to Americans' daring dreams: the first suspension bridge, the first animated film, the first twenty-four-hour news network, the fastest man, the lightest cellular phone.

Even in Las Vegas, I feel the power of the American dream. Where else could there be such a tourist attraction in the middle of the desert?

Of course, sometimes dreamers just end up as day-dreamers or reckless risk takers. However, once one lands in America, one cannot help but dream. Opportunities are given to those who seek them. In America, there is a spirit of hope and possibility that cannot easily be found in other countries. As someone once said, "All you need is a dollar and a dream." Americans dream big dreams, and dreams build America.

Frontier Spirit

Americans' frontier spirit can be summarized in *Star Trek's* mission: "To explore strange new worlds; to seek out new life and new civilizations; to boldly go where no one has gone before." The American frontier spirit led settlers to the wild west and later around the globe. Admiral Robert E. Peary discovered the North Pole in 1909; in 1927 Charles Lindbergh made the first solo crossing of the Atlantic to Paris; American businesspeople are exploring the globe from Vietnam to Russia, selling American images, products, and services. The list could fill a book. The launching and success of the National Geographic Society are testimony to Americans' relentless pursuit of the unknown world, inner or outer. The founders had one goal in mind: to promote the "increase and diffusion of geographical knowledge." The society's *National Geographic* magazine has served as "the window to the world" to millions of Americans and non-Americans, and the organization offers memberships in 170 countries.

Thanks to Americans' spirit of exploration, people are no longer earthbound. Who can forget the images of the *Apollo* astronauts on the moon? It was "one small step for man; one giant leap for mankind." Since going to the moon, Americans have been actively exploring outer space. When they are physically limited in their ability to explore the solar system, they let their imaginations explore the unknown frontiers. The *Star Trek* series and *Star Wars* movies are an extension of this country's quest to explore the unknown. Furthermore, Americans have endeavored to conquer the inner space of the human body. America is the leader in brain research and psychology, searching for new ways of healing and improving the human mind.

Charles Kettering, the engineer who developed the first electric cash register, said, "Where there is an open mind, there will always be a frontier." This adventurous spirit has enabled Americans to expand the frontiers of human knowledge, especially in science. From university research laboratories to government think tanks to Silicon Valley start-up companies, Americans are not afraid to experiment with new ideas. It is no accident that Nobel laureates in chemistry, physics, and physiology and medicine are often from the United States. The late David Sarnoff, a pioneer in the development of radio and television broadcasting, credited freedom and liberty for America's superiority in the sciences: "Freedom is the oxygen without which science cannot breathe."

Thriving on this free spirit, Americans desire to reach out and touch the world—and change it. The American communications system has altered the way people connect with each other. Many of the world's greatest inven-

anesthesia

Otis!

Nylon

Bill
Gates

tions are credited to Americans, from the telephone to the computer. Anesthesia, the miracle of painless surgery, is among the greatest gifts that American medicine has given to humanity. The invention of the safety device on passenger elevators by Elisha Otis in 1852 led to the construction of skyscrapers and encouraged metropolitan growth around the world. Nylon, the first man-made synthetic fiber, invented by the du Pont company, has forever changed the lives of people around the world. The impact of Bill Gates' MS-DOS is not even measurable.

Some attribute Americans' genius to their ability to question, to think critically and creatively. Professor Chin Ning Yang, a Chinese American Nobel laureate in physics, related the experience of some of his students from China and Taiwan. "Professor Yang," they would say to him, "I find it very strange that I was among the best in my class in examinations, but now that I am doing research work, the American students are much more lively, much better than I am." Yang believes that despite the criticism of the American educational system, it produces highly creative individuals. Now Yang encourages his Asians students to explore: "You may see only vaguely what is going on, but you should not be afraid of that. That was one of the things I learned after I came to this country [America]." Indeed, it is incredible that 29 percent of Silicon Valley CEOs were born in Asia. Some even say that Silicon Valley is now called "IC Valley" due to its Indian and Chinese population. What would have happened to them had they not come to the United States? Certainly, Americans' belief in the promise of the unexpected, the willingness to "boldly go where no one has gone before," has encouraged people with new ideas to experiment. While some Asian countries lament their brain drain to the U.S., others recognize that the brains would have been wasted if their owners had stayed in their own countries.

Michael A. Ledeen, a resident scholar at the American Enterprise Institute, wrote in his book *Tocqueville on American Character*:

> The clever masquerade cloaks the basic tension between our passion for personal fulfillment and our mission to create heaven on earth. We are simultaneously driven in both directions, which is why we insist on limited government and maximum individual freedom but also demand vigorous action from the government to assist them in their efforts. It is the usual, amazing balancing act, a high-wire tour de force.[3]

Recently, Asian countries have been changing their schools' curricula to produce more original thinkers. They have also been trying to promote a spirit of exploration and discovery among their citizens. Silicon Valley's success has been an inspiration to both entrepreneurs and mandarins in Asia. However, despite the math and science competency of Asian schoolchildren, Nobel Prizes will continue to elude them until they are taught to be curious about the unknown and to ask why, even about the seemingly obvious. More importantly, Asian bureaucrats should look more closely at the role of limited government and an open system that allows for unknown ventures.

Seeing Everybody as Equal

An Asian visitor was coming out of a convenience store and saw a homeless man digging in a trash dumpster. He felt sorry for the homeless man and went back to the store and bought two sandwiches for him. When he handed them to the man, the man offered to shake his donor's hand and said, "Thank you. God bless you." This gesture shocked the Asian man, because the homeless man seemed to assume equality with his benefactor. Although this may have been an isolated incident, for the Asian visitor it was a reminder of the American belief in a classless society. In America, class is not one's birthright.

In the American workplace, most people make their own coffee and clean up their own desks. The person who takes the last cup from the pot refills it. This act may seem trivial, but behind it lies a philosophy of equality. In Asia, people who serve and people who are served belong to different classes. Customers treat servers with no respect, as if they belong to a lower class. They often use a commanding tone of voice and even yell at servers if the service is not satisfactory. In the United States, waiters and store clerks regard themselves as equals with their customers; they exchange jokes and pleasantries with customers. Secretaries do not feel that they have to meet the personal needs of their bosses and are not afraid to voice their opinions.

In Asia, people are often treated differently based on family background, occupation, the school one attended, and geographic origin. Asians are always interested in their status in relation to others. In Confucian tradition, there are the rulers and the ruled. Confucianism saw all human relations in the light of vertical relationships: upper classes always wielded authority, and lower classes always obeyed authority. Ordinary citizens could not assert any rights against government agencies. Officials had undisputed authority over businesses and civilians. Under the tradition, inferiors were supposed to behave with deference toward their superiors and not challenge their authority. In a family, this meant that wives were to submit to their husbands and that young people were to submit to their elders. Everyone was born with a designated status. Even when twins were born, the firstborn was awarded a higher status and inherited more than the second.

Twins

The inequality of Confucian tradition has hindered the implementation of justice in Asian societies, because the laws and rules are applied differently depending on a person's status in society. The "haves" have connections and privileges that are not available to the "have-nots." Thus, political leaders and their relatives are rarely indicted or investigated for possible wrongdoing while they are in office. Some argue that even in the United States, one's ability to afford a good lawyer decides guilt or innocence, but at least poor Americans are not denied justice completely. In some Asian countries, cases against the powerful are rarely revealed to the public and are often dismissed behind the scenes. Even simple rules such as waiting in line can be observed or ignored based on one's status and connections.

In contrast, in America, everybody—regardless of his or her status and connections—can expect equal treatment by law. In most places, people observe the first come, first served rule. Blue-collar and white-collar workers are equally proud of their professions. Employers cannot fire employees without due process. Superiors do not demand duties unrelated to their subordinates' jobs. Although there are still cases of nepotism and personal favoritism in the United States, Americans clearly have more opportunities to gain a level playing field than Asians do.

Of course, there is a price for taking equality to its extreme. By always thinking "I am just as good as the next person," no matter what their experience, Americans miss opportunities to learn from people who are indeed more successful or at least more experienced or educated than they are. Americans have a naive way of believing that no one is superior to them. With that belief, they abandon vertical principles, traditions, hierarchies, and obligations that could be positive in guiding younger generations. In Asia, it is common for elders, supervisors, and professors to give life instructions to their juniors or students without being asked. They assume the responsibility of sharing with their juniors the wisdom that only age or experience can teach. In America, even loving parents are often afraid to give advice to children. Out of fear of offending them, some parents forgo the opportunity to guide their children. Another negative side effect of equality is lack of decorum. Many young Americans call elders by their first names and act informally, sometimes even rudely.

Nevertheless, given this egalitarian spirit, Americans enjoy at least somewhat equal opportunity outside of the workplace as well. In Asian countries, the leisure activities of white-collar and blue-collar workers are drastically different. For example, playing golf is prohibitively expensive; club memberships can cost tens of thousands of dollars or more. But in America, many firefighters, schoolteachers, and factory workers play golf regularly. In America, people with less money may play at public golf courses or stay at less expensive ski resorts, but at least they have the opportunity to enjoy the same kinds of leisure activities as the rich.

One recent newcomer to the United States said, "People come to America because America is an ideal. There's no other country in the history of the world that people want to go to so much in their hearts, not just because of money, but because of what the ideal says: everyone is created equal." Since the founding fathers' days, Americans have sought to give everybody a chance—a fair opportunity to achieve regardless of age, gender, race, background, or religious preference. Although the reality falls short of the ideal, the effort toward the ideal is what makes America unique. With all its imperfections, America has a clearer view of equality than almost any other country.

Daring to Be Yourself

Like all other people in the world, Americans are concerned with peer pressure and public image; yet they tend to care less about what other people think than Asians do. Individual identity or preference often overrules social expectations and conformity. Even ordinary people yearn to be different and feel special. According to nineteenth-century French historian Alexis de Tocqueville, this is due to American democracy. As social conditions have become more equal, more people have acquired sufficient education and financial means to satisfy their wants. They owe nothing to anyone and expect nothing from anyone. Since they consider themselves to be standing alone, they feel that they can be unique.

For Americans, being true to oneself is first and foremost. Thus, Americans continually search for their individual identities and insist on others' recognition of their different interests, styles, and preferences. Thanks to a society that values diversity, Americans can express individuality and uniqueness in every aspect of their lives. Anyone who wants to change hair color or clothing style can do so. Many people not only furnish and decorate their homes to reflect their personality but also custom-design their houses. They express themselves through their lawns and gardens and the color of their walls. Advertisements for merchandise mirror the American psyche, such as the "I am" theme in a Levi's jeans commercial. One of the highest compliments one American can pay another about hairstyle, clothing, or even a car is, "That's really you!"

In America, self-expression is inculcated from an early age. Children are encouraged to express themselves through school papers, plays, clothing, hairstyles, room decorations, and many other means. Adopting "No Fear" as their slogan, young people feel free to make their own statements in various ways and to grow into unique and creative individuals. It is no accident that creativity in worldwide entertainment has been dominated by American legends such as Walt Disney, George Lucas, Steven Spielberg, and Madonna.

In Asia, it is not as easy to find individuals with a strong sense of self. Their identity is strongly influenced by family and group expectations. Although the younger generation wants to claim more independence, a group mentality still dominates. Traditionally, Asians tend to reward conformity and restrict individuality. Three hundred fifty million people in China have the same five surnames: Li, Wang, Zhang, Liu, and Chen. In Korea, three surnames, Kim, Lee, and Park, are shared by 45 percent of the population. In many Asian companies, employees still wear uniforms. When Japanese businessmen go out in a group, they often order the same dish, usually following the lead of their superior.

This kind of conformity is reinforced from early ages. Some Asian children are not allowed to choose even the length of their hair or the color of their shoes; these choices are made for them first by parents, and later by school administrators. Lee O-Young, author of *Smaller Is Better*, wrote that Japan is a kind of totalitarian state that forces its entire population to fit into a small framework, just as food is reduced and packed into a *bento* (lunch box). Their forms and shapes as individuals are preset by social influences. It is little wonder that Japanese children take group acceptance so seriously. In Japan, there have been many cases of elementary and middle school students committing suicide over not being accepted by the group.

For centuries, Asians have valued group harmony and conformity. The individual was not as important as the group. People's identities were determined by the groups they belonged to. Superiority did not arise from being exceptional but rather from conforming to the established norms. Right actions were defined by Confucian traditions in terms of one's duties and obligations. If one didn't live up to the norms, one was labeled an unnatural and abnormal person who didn't fit into society. Consequently, in the words of an Asian proverb, even today, "The nail that sticks out gets hammered down." Individuals have to continually adjust to well-defined traditional rules and roles. This kind of mentality kills the seed of creativity. Although there are many Asian musicians studying at the Julliard School, Asia has produced only a few master performers. Interestingly, the few Asians who have achieved international prominence, such as violinist Midori, cellist Yo-Yo Ma, and conductor Chung Myung Hoon, began their training in the United States at an early age. The principal weakness of Asian performers seems to be that many do not express their emotions as openly or as freely as their Western counterparts.

Recently, Asian schools and companies have been trying to encourage individuality among students and employees in the hope that it will improve their creativity. But those with a strong individualistic orientation are not always appreciated by their peers. If someone dares to be different or pulls ahead of the pack, he or she will be labeled a renegade, and a collective effort will be made to discredit that person. Even in rapidly changing China, those with special training or talents who don't fit the standard Chinese mold are often subjected to criticism and other forms of discrimination by their fellow workers, simply because they act differently. Given such intolerance for uniqueness, many Asians do not think it worthwhile to express individuality. As someone said, "A Chinese tends to mobilize his thought and action for the purpose of conforming to the reality, while an American tends to do so for the purpose of making the reality conform to him." Thus, the individualists in Asia are waging silent and often lonely battles against conformist traditions.

Individual Merit

An American human resources manager at an Asian subsidiary wanted to hire an applicant for a sales position. The manager recommended the applicant to his Asian supervisor because he valued the applicant's work experience. The potential employee had worked throughout college, holding several part-time positions while in school. Yet the boss disapproved of the candidate based on his background. "If a person had to support his own education, he must have come from a poor family, and he can't have the right connections to sell our products. Nor can he be trusted with company money." This was his rationale.

Asian employers often look at an applicant's family background, school, region, and religion as part of their screening process. When a friend of mine with a Ph.D. in microbiology applied for a faculty position in Korea, the interviewers asked the professions of her father, her husband, and her father-in-law. Employers in Asia use personal information to assess whether a potential employee can be trusted, will bring any valuable connections to the company, or will be loyal to the employer. Many of these practices would be illegal in the United States, where all employers strive to provide equal opportunity. Although connections and networking are important in American businesses, an individual's merit plays a bigger role in getting a job or being promoted than in Asian countries.

In Asian cultures, individual recognition is inseparable from the webs of relationships. Where everyone is intertwined, the sense of self is an interdependent, group-oriented concept. For example, the Chinese term *guanxi* (interlocking relationship patterns) conveys who knows whom and who is in charge of whom. The worth of an individual continues to be measured in social terms. One of my Asian friends, an assistant professor in the United States who was up for tenure, commented on the review process: "I expect a fairer evaluation here than in my home country. There are reviews by my peers across the country, and they are pretty objective." She knows that in her own country she would have to spend more time lobbying for her tenure than doing research in her field, because relationships outweigh individual merit.

Asians' focus on connections often creates a pattern of corruption and nepotism. Life can be challenging for those who do not have the right ties to families, companies, schools, and officials. Although many Asian countries are moving toward valuing individual merit, the lower classes have limited opportunities for upward mobility, because significant cultural changes can take a few generations. Many Asian enterprises are family owned, so father, sons, sons-in-law, nephews, cousins, and other close relatives play decisive roles in managing an enterprise. School and regional ties often last a lifetime and affect one's career and business.

Family background also affects Asians' personal lives. Many Asian parents still select or recommend mates for their children, often scrutinizing the family backgrounds of their children's would-be partners and determining their worth based on the parents' social status and wealth. Wealthy parents are eager to enhance their own connections through their children's marriages. They use marriage as a convenient method of making strategic alliances with certain families. In Korea, for example, the marriage network of the rich and powerful is so vast that a group of reporters published a 448-page book on these relationships. Marriages have connected many business conglomerates, as well as former presidents, prime ministers, and politicians. If Bill Gates had been in Korea when he was single, he would have been pressured to marry a woman with political connections.

It is unfortunate that in Asia a person's life is often determined by factors other than individual merit. To be an ideal candidate for marriage, a potential mate must come from the right family, one with a good reputation and without any "defects" or skeletons in the closet. For example, if a young man has a disabled family member, this fact may be used against him. If one's parents are divorced, that is another negative factor. If either of a person's parents is deceased, that can be another drawback, because Asians believe that the absence of one parent may cause a lack of proper education and upbringing. In extreme cases, the marriage plans of lovers can be terminated simply because the hour and date of a potential mate's birth are unfavorable. It is not fair that people have to take responsibility for factors they cannot choose. No matter how good one may be, one can be penalized for one's background.

In contrast, Americans are far more likely to accept others regardless of their parents' marital status or disabilities in the family. In America, what counts is who you are, not who others around you are. A person tends to be judged on his or her own merit. Unfortunately, discrimination does exist in America, and total equality has yet to be achieved. Although the law prohibits discrimination on the basis of race, color, religion, national origin, age, or disability, many still experience discrimination because of such factors. Some also argue that affirmative action has hindered America's merit-based system because gender and race can now override merit. Nevertheless, America is surely one of the best places for people with merit and strong motivation to reach their potential.

Separation of Personal and Professional

One of the first things Americans need to know to do business in Asia is the importance of building relationships. In many Asian countries, the distinction between personal and professional relationships is blurred. Thus, when someone has a good relationship with a person in power, he or she can easily negotiate a favorable deal or cut through red tape. Even special restrictions can be ignored. Susan Au Allen, president of the U.S.–Pan Asian American Chamber of Commerce in Washington, said, "China is not ruled by law, but ruled by people who make the law. There is a difference. The people can make up the law and change it anytime they want. Therefore, there is no law."

In many Asian countries, people perceive the law as a guideline. In Indonesia, for example, the former president's children were awarded numerous lucrative joint-venture deals. Thus, when the Asian economic crisis hit the region in 1997, the Western media cited "crony capitalism" as the main reason, and a *Wall Street Journal* editorial questioned, "Is corruption an Asian value?" It is definitely an overgeneralization to say that nepotism and corruption are Asian values. Singapore has maintained a spotlessly clean government under the leadership of the founding father and former prime minister Lee Kuan Yew. By paying public servants high salaries and implementing tough laws against bribery, he was able to prevent corruption. "You owe a duty to your family and loyalty to your friends, to help and support them. But you must do that from your private resources, not public resources," said Lee. With the exception of Singapore, when people in Asia mix personal relationships with professional ones, nepotism and corruption often prosper.

According to Lucian W. Pye, in the past Chinese children learned the importance of establishing favorable relationships in order to escape from authority. Growing up in extended-family households, they learned that one way to get around monolithic authority was through fostering personal ties, such as a special relationship with a powerful or respected aunt, uncle, or grandparent. Pye argued in his book, *Asian Power and Politics*, "Children understood quickly that authority could have whim and there was always the off chance that authority could be 'bribed' to be more tolerant." Although Asians increasingly live in nuclear-family units, children still learn the importance of personal relationships in getting what they want.

This emphasis on personal relationships produces elaborate calculations of mutual obligations. In elections, people often vote for candidates who have direct ties to them as personal friends, former classmates, or relatives. If they don't have such connections, they may vote for someone from the same hometown. Many are extremely loyal to their relationships and are not swayed by candidates' merits or by the issues; rather, they are governed by norms of reciprocity. In Korea and Taiwan, until recently, it was common for candidates to entertain voters or send gifts to them before the election to create an obligation to return these gifts as votes. Politicians also know that when they are elected, they owe favors to these voters. Out of fear of losing face, they find ways to return them.

Unlike Asians, Americans are usually able to separate business situations from personal interests. In the United States, rules are rules, and they are applied universally regardless of connections. Although exceptions exist, they are rare. People cannot expect favors because of connections. Government officials refuse to give special deals or inside information to their family and friends. College professors do not use different evaluation standards for their favorite students or for the children of friends; students have to earn the grades themselves. Schoolteachers are expected to treat children relatively the same, regardless of the students' socioeconomic backgrounds or the parents' involvement in school. In America, gifts from parents don't make a difference in a child's report card, but in Asia, a lot of parents give gifts to teachers to solicit special treatment for their children.

In the U.S. workplace, a person doesn't get special favors from his or her boss because they went to the same school or are from the same town. Workers do not have obligations to their supervisors that are not related to their jobs. In Asia, good employees are often willing to do personal errands for their bosses—and more. A friend of mine in Asia told me that everyone in her office had loaned as much as three thousand dollars to their office chief, and some people had even cosigned a loan application for the boss because of his credit limit. They were afraid that if they refused, they would disrupt office harmony. This would be unthinkable for Americans. Asian workers also have to be conscious of their status outside work. For example, it is politically incorrect to drive a more expensive car than the boss. Even children are aware of the relative status of their fathers when they play.

Because Asians are involved in their work, in the endless cycle of obligations, and in the constant search for useful connections, they rarely get a break from work. An Asian businessman who returned home after a stint in the United States complained about the lack of personal time in his country. "My life is structured regardless of my wishes. My schedule is full with engagements I would rather not attend but must honor in order to stay in business." In Asia, most employees are expected to drink and dine with their co-workers or clients after work hours. There have been cases in which corporate employees died from alcohol poisoning trying to fulfill what they saw as their obligations. The job of entertaining clients after work is limited in America, and most people can spend their evenings as they wish. In America, everybody is entitled to a personal life.

Of course, personal and professional relationships can become enmeshed in the United States, too, resulting in nepotism and favoritism. People in power exercise their influence to make deals for their friends. It is merely a matter of degree. Yet, U.S. corporations have rules to guard against favoritism. Some companies prohibit their suppliers or vendors from buying gifts or meals for their clients. Some require their employees to report any gift worth over twenty-five dollars; others have strict guidelines for giving or accepting gifts. While harmonious human relationships are important, when we separate the personal from the professional, we enjoy each on its own merit and encourage fairness for everybody.

Competitive Spirit

"Winning isn't everything—it's the only thing," said legendary Green Bay Packers coach Vince Lombardi. Many people believe that sports have had a positive influence on American society, and the competitive nature of sports has provided Americans with many metaphors. Businesspeople often use sports terms and expressions in their speech, such as "playing in the big league," "strike out," "slam-dunk," and "touchdown." For competitive Americans, who hate losing, everything in life is a game to win. Their love of competition is reflected in their obsession with ratings and rankings. Nowhere have I seen so many ratings: the best cities to do business in, the best places to raise children, the best colleges and universities, the cities with the cleanest air, the one hundred richest people, the twenty-five most beautiful people, the fifty most influential people, the sixty most intriguing people, the sexiest man in America, and many more.

In its purest form, competition challenges Americans to become better. In 1994 and 1995, the United States climbed to the top of the list of the world's most competitive economies, displacing Japan for the first time since 1985, according to the annual global survey conducted by the Geneva-based World Economic Forum. Prior to 1994, when Japan had the lead, Americans criticized themselves harshly for failing to be number one; they did not quietly accept defeat in world economic leadership.

Looking out for number one, Americans love to compete on and off the job. On the job, there is competition for market share, profitability, customer satisfaction, promotion, on-time delivery, and best-in-class performance. "We'll not tolerate losing. Our company is about winning," reads a corporate mission statement. American performance evaluation systems force employees to perform. From CEOs to factory workers, there is no guaranteed work unless people prove their worth. Many divisions of vertically integrated U.S. companies have to compete against outside vendors to sell their products to the other divisions of their own companies. They have to compete with regard to quality, price, service, and delivery time. In Asia, a subsidiary of a major conglomerate does not have to sell hard within the group. It knows that the other subsidiaries must use its products, regardless of external factors. This kind of protectionism doesn't help either customers or companies. It only encourages mediocrity.

Competition has brought the best prices and the best customer service to American consumers. In fact, Wal-Mart's arrival in Europe has shaken up European retailers with its stiff competition and lower prices. Regarding customer service, one German worker said that American companies work extremely hard to please the toughest customers in the world. If some Americans think that they are getting poor customer service, they should travel abroad. For example, many Americans in France have learned that the customer is always wrong. Common U.S. practices, including the no-questions-asked return policy and the lowest price guaran-

Customers = unquestioned return policy

tee, are not easily found elsewhere. Customers cannot expect to receive credit from a long-distance telephone carrier for questionable calls on their bills. In America, there is an implicit belief that customers tell the truth. Although some abuse the honor system, Americans enjoy "enlightened consumerism"; the customer is king.

No doubt competition has produced for the United States some of the best professionals, the best products, and the best business practices in the world. Nevertheless, there is a downside to Americans' emphasis on winning at any cost. The pressure to win can be overwhelming in America, where only winners are cheered and remembered and the winner takes all, including multimillion-dollar advertising contracts. Tonya Harding, the figure skater who arranged to have her Olympic competitor, Nancy Kerrigan, injured, is an extreme example of the pressure to win. The overemphasis on competition also contributes to a hostile workplace. Employees constantly compete against their peers and lose sleep over who gets credit for a new sales plan or for having the best ideas; this discourages teamwork and strains human relations. At school, cheating has become a serious concern when even the top students do it regularly.

Asians believe that it is neither necessary nor beneficial to be obsessed with winning. Although they set goals for surpassing their previous achievements and emphasize doing their personal best, when it comes to competing with others, Asians choose their battles carefully. They consider the cost of winning, not materially but emotionally and socially. In human relations, many Asians believe that it is better to promote peace and harmony than to win at any cost. It is dangerous to think that if one is not a winner, one must be a loser. Some may look like losers at first, but they may turn out to be winners in the long run. As Lao Tzu said in *Tao Te Ching*, "In natural law, some lose and yet profit along the way. Some profit and yet lose along their way."

Therefore, if Americans work toward viewing their competitive spirit from a more balanced perspective, they will learn to appreciate the courage to fail and to be graceful in failure. A few decades ago, General Douglas MacArthur prayed, "Build me a son who will be proud and unbending in honest defeat and humble and gentle in victory." Americans need this prayer so that they can be content with winning or losing after giving their all.

Systematic Planning and Organization

"I'm so organized, it's almost scary," reads an advertisement for the Franklin Quest organizers. Americans have mastered the art of planning and organizing, as reflected in highways, streets, national parks, conventions, megastore aisles, grocery shelves, and support groups. After traveling around the world, I have concluded that American highways are wonderful. They are well laid out, and the directions are clear and easy to follow (most of the time). Street signs and numbers are arranged systematically, making it easy to find an address. In many Asian countries, it is extremely difficult to find an address because there is no apparent method for assigning street names and numbers. At national parks across the United States, from Alaska to Hawaii, services and information are consistent. There are visitor centers, park rangers, guided tours, well-marked roads, and information brochures. At shopping malls, customers can predict what they will find in certain shops, regardless of which city they are in. At megastores and supermarkets, customers can easily find the products they need, because everything is displayed in a systematic order and in different sizes and colors, with signs above each aisle to identify what you will find there. In Asia, shoppers have to visit many different stores and rely on the whims of the shop owners, who organize the shelves according to their own preferences.

American education also uses a systems approach, with three elements: input, process, and output. I have heard that this instructional system was originally developed for military training during World War II. With that tradition, all educational materials and training manuals have specific learning objectives and outcomes and include detailed processes to accomplish them. Many management tools and training systems are packaged and marketed for hefty prices. Even many of the best-selling self-help books include exercises and have sequel workbooks for those who want to systematically implement the lessons from their reading.

Americans learn early how to gather and organize information. The lessons learned in any process are carefully documented and transferred to the next person who can benefit from that information. This practice produces specialists in very narrow areas, creating the most unusual job titles—alarm investigator, pedestrian coordinator, parking analyst, life strategist, diversity manager, lactation consultant, and so on. In contrast, for most Asians, information is only in the heads of the people who are involved. For example, the best cooks and chefs often don't have recipes for their special dishes. "Just add some soy sauce and pepper until it tastes good" is their advice for those who want to prepare a gourmet dish.

The American penchant for systematic planning is also shown in the itemization of bills. A phone bill, for example, details all the charges, and includes the time and duration of each call. At auto body shops, the tasks to be performed are itemized along with the cost of materials. Even for pest control services, bills list the types of insects exterminated and the amount of pesticide used. In many other countries, customers see only the final charges; for example, a repair person will give a customer a final bill, with nothing that verifies the work done.

Reporting for *Time* magazine in 1999, Andrew Ferguson wrote that America is a country that systemizes everything:

> We create seminars on how to make friends, teach classes in grieving and make pet walking a profession.... So if our children are to have sports, we will make leagues and teams, write schedules and rule books, publish box scores and rankings, hire coaches and refs, buy uniforms and equipment to the limit of our means.[4]

Americans even have systems to manage volunteer activities, nonprofit associations, and personal hobbies. A few years ago, I went to Fort Collins, Colorado, on business. Upon arriving at the hotel, I found large crowds of people, so I asked another hotel guest what was going on. She answered that it was a national convention of rose growers. Since then, I have found that there are all kinds of conventions—for hobbyists, bird-watchers, and miniature doll collectors. It is not an accident that Martha Stewart has become the American queen of home improvement. Her organizational ability is beyond my comprehension, but there are many followers who approach their home projects with weekly and monthly planning schedules.

Of course, there is always the possibility of overdoing it. As much as I appreciate order, I don't envy those Americans who are so organized. I can't see much use for organizers for time, space, tools, seasonings, coupons, and even pregnancy. These things are supposed to simplify my life, but they are too complicated for a simple-minded Asian like me. Even self-help workshops and tools designed to help one achieve simplicity are too much for me, because the American process of simplifying is so meticulously planned and organized.

I like the way most Asians live: one day at a time. They have no specific system to prioritize lists. Many do not have time management systems. Most people answer all their phone calls when they are in the office. When personal friends call, they take the time to talk to them as long as they want. Asia has produced many outstanding people who have achieved personal and professional success, but maybe Asians would have been more productive or successful if they had been more organized. But why should they? Many Asians are content and enjoy glorious meals prepared without recipes.

Flexible Systems, Flexible Roles

Free-spirited Americans believe in the flexibility of their systems. Take higher education, for example. One of the best higher education systems in the world is available when a young (or older) person is ready. He or she can skip a year before going to college or take time off before finishing college. In America, graduating from college within four years is no longer the norm. More and more college students take five years to graduate, because many work their way through school or take time off. Tiger Woods, the youngest golfer to win the Masters, summarized this flexible spirit: "I made a commitment to my parents that I would finish college so long as I didn't have a time limit. Whether I do it in five years or fifteen is up to me, but I will finish." Taking time off is often beneficial. Many peak performers took time off to wonder and wander when they were young. After their soul- and goal-searching process, they returned with a clearer direction for their lives.

Once they enter college, American students are not restricted to one school or one major. They can change schools and majors as often as they want, whereas Asian students cannot easily do so. James Michener, the late Pulitzer Prize-winning author, revealed that he was encouraged to attend nine universities and centers of learning at the public's expense.

In many Asian countries, it is extremely difficult to get into college because of the stringent entrance examination process, and it is almost impossible to put off college for a few years after high school graduation. No matter how hard they work in high school, about three-fourths of students fail their college entrance examinations and lose the chance to get a degree. Although they can retake these exams year after year, the chance of passing them grow slimmer every year. To make matters worse, Asians have limited opportunities to pursue advanced education of any kind and to start professional careers. Adults returning to college, especially the college of their choice, are almost nonexistent.

Job opportunities are also flexible in America. Americans don't feel stuck in their first careers. An actor can become the president, and a lawyer can become a best-selling novelist. A general can switch careers and be a motivational speaker, and a corporate executive can become a high school teacher. People also have side jobs that are completely different from their main jobs: a teacher works at a department store during the summer; a church choir director works as a librarian while pursuing his law degree; an artist works as a chef. Without feeling restricted by their backgrounds, Americans are ready to take advantage of the opportunities that are open to them.

In Asian countries, changing careers is difficult, and changing employers can be equally challenging. Although young Asians are increasingly willing to change employers for more money and better opportunities, they are still in the minority. And once Asians reach their midforties, they have very limited opportunities to reinvent themselves by going back to school or pursuing second careers.

Americans apply their flexibility to personal pursuits as well. A banker might play in a band at a bar during weekends, or an MIT-educated research scientist might teach an evening dance class. Americans follow their passions. If they can afford to take extended time off, they may become lay missionaries or serve as Peace Corps volunteers in developing countries. Others travel the world just to explore.

This flexible spirit is positively transferred to social organizations and business management. Many companies

allow employees flexible work hours. Managers often introduce cross-functional teams to their organizations for special projects. Pastors are flexible enough to cancel evening
services on Super Bowl Sunday to allow members to join the
rest of the country in watching a football game. Church
buildings are turned into soup kitchens to feed the hungry
during the week; libraries are used for support-group meetings in the evenings.

These flexible systems allow Americans to move from
one role to another with little conflict. They wear different
hats for different tasks. On occasion top executives serve
food during company-sponsored luncheons to express their
appreciation to their employees. Men and women blur their
traditional roles. Men do not necessarily feel unmanly
when they cook for their wives, and women do not feel
unfeminine when they change a tire or mow the lawn. In
fact, the number of househusbands is steadily increasing.
This flexibility allows Americans to see others as equals
with whom they can empathize, based on common experience. In Asia, gender roles are more clearly defined. There
are few husbands who are willing to take care of the
housework.

Each American, then, writes his or her own script. And
one doesn't have to pay a steep price for marching to the
beat of one's own drum.

Empowerment of Women

"There are two kinds of women in the world: American
women and women." This is a joke among Asian men doing
business internationally. American women have been liber-

ated and empowered to such a degree that they belong in a category all their own among the women of the world. Compared with their counterparts in other countries, American women have accomplished a great deal in career advancement. Even European nations that maintain progressive, family-oriented programs lag far behind the United States in providing equal employment opportunities to women. In Japan, Germany, and other European and Asian countries, women face serious obstacles to achieving workplace equality. They are expected to assist men and are given lower wages, less stable employment, and fewer opportunities for advancement.

American women still have a long way to go for completely equal compensation and top management positions, but there is some evidence that the glass ceiling is breaking. Carly Fiorina, CEO of Hewlett-Packard; Andrea Chung, CEO of Avon; Debby Hopkins, CFO of Lucent; Shelly Lazarus, CEO of Ogilvy & Mather; and Sherry Lansing, Chair of the Motion Picture Group of Paramount Pictures are a few of the top female executives in corporate America. Although only 3 to 5 percent of senior positions are currently held by women, they account for 43 percent of the nation's executives, administrators, and managers. No other country has such a record of progress. Women in America have access to almost any field and can excel as professionals. Madeleine Albright, former secretary of state, and Judith Rodin, president of the University of Pennsylvania, prove that no job is off-limits to women. As they gain experience, more and more women will rise to top-level jobs.

In Asia, the law may require employers to give equal opportunities to women, but even the best-educated women face discrimination when seeking employment. Male interviewers tend to favor male applicants because men are supposed to be the breadwinners in the family. In China, business and government organizations usually hire men before women, figuring that men will not require paid maternity leave or days off to deal with family affairs. Once they get jobs, Asian women must deal with the sexist attitudes of Asian men and must tolerate unpleasant remarks or pass unusual tests. Even in the late 1990s, some female job candidates in Japan were told by male interviewers that the company needed good-looking women. During the interview, they had to put up with such sexist comments as "If only you wore a shorter skirt." In Korea in 1994, forty-four major corporations were sued for imposing weight and height restrictions on women as criteria for employment. The companies specified in their advertisements that female applicants should be between five feet and five feet, four inches tall and should weigh 130 pounds or less. Even if they pass such tests, women in Asia are likely to face other obstacles related to sexism that American women don't have to deal with.

In traditional Confucian society, men and women were supposed to have different statuses and roles. Women could not even attend some family functions with their husbands; such ceremonies were closed to them. They were not allowed to offer sacrifices, burn incense, offer food and wine, or bow before their ancestors. Also, a woman was supposed to be loyal to three men in her life—her father when she was young, her husband when she was married, and her son when she was old. This tradition of sexism is prevalent throughout Asia, despite a growing women's movement. An American executive who returned from a three-month assignment in Japan told me of his discomfort over having coffee served by office ladies. The office ladies in Japan, who make up the majority of all clerical workers, are expected to make tea, serve snacks, clean desks, and perform other domestic tasks in addition to fulfilling their secretarial duties.

Furthermore, in Confucian tradition, women could not interrupt men's conversations or speak loudly or be aggressive. Women were told, "If a hen cries, the family will disintegrate." Many Asian women still do not assert their rights at home or at work. Asian men tend to resent assertive women, and Asian women are afraid of offending their men. Many Japanese women still speak in a higher-than-natural pitch (for social acceptance), especially in formal settings, on the phone, or when dealing with customers. Supposedly, Japanese men are attracted to high-pitched voices; they perceive women with lower voices as too aggressive or unfeminine.

America has its male chauvinists, but it certainly has a more enlightened male population when it comes to empowering women. Although American women may not be completely satisfied with their status in society and at home, they can be proud of what they have achieved. American women are fortunate to live in a society that allows the wives of presidential candidates to share the podium with their husbands at national conventions and to talk about national issues. In Asia, the wives of presidential candidates would not dare speak their minds, for fear of offending the voters. American women have set the standard for women in other countries with this message: prove your worth and declare your independence.

With continued progress for American women, one downside I see is the lack of appreciation for women who choose homemaking as a full-time career. While the society admires and praises successful career women, there is little glory or recognition for homemakers' important and difficult job. Although homemakers don't make that choice in the hope of receiving recognition, Americans can make homemakers feel proud of their choice if they see working inside the home as rewarding and fulfilling.

Releasing Human Potential

A few months after I came to America, one of my American friends showed me a picture of her sister. "Isn't she precious?" she said. I was taken aback; her sister had Down's syndrome. On another occasion, when I first met my new neighbor, she revealed that she had a mentally retarded son who was sixteen but had the mental capacity of a five-year-old. I admire Americans' openness about disability. Many Americans are not ashamed of having a mentally or physically disabled family member. On the contrary, some people advocate for the disabled to protect their rights and to educate the public. The Kennedy family is one example. Eunice Kennedy, sister of former president John F. Kennedy, established the Kennedy Mental Retardation Foundation in honor of her mentally retarded sister.

This kind of acceptance and openness has inspired

people with disabilities to dare to fulfill their potential. Despite being deaf, mute, and blind, Helen Keller became a brilliant author and educator. With the help of her devoted teacher, Annie Sullivan, Keller became happy and productive. Heather Whitestone, Miss America of 1995, is deaf, yet she was able to win a prestigious pageant and motivate others. Keller and Whitestone were able to accomplish what they did because they were born in America. At my gym, I once saw a disabled gentleman wearing a T-shirt with a message that summarized Americans' acceptance of disabilities. "I may not be perfect, but some parts of my body are excellent." Americans celebrate the wholeness of some parts, rather than expecting the perfection of all of them.

Americans' acceptance of disability is reflected not only in their attitudes but in their building construction as well. Most American buildings give access to the physically disabled, and many are equipped with wheelchair ramps and elevator floor numbers in Braille. Most public toilets provide access to people in wheelchairs, and automated auditory directions are often given for the benefit of the visually impaired. These things are not easily found in buildings in Asia, where disabled people are not fully accepted.

I am grateful for my American experience, because it has taught me to accept people with different abilities. I now look for their potential and don't pity them. When I was pregnant, I was advised to have amniocentesis because of my age. I was told that I had a greater chance than younger women of having a baby with Down's syndrome or other disabilities and that the test would reveal such imperfections in the embryo. I decided not to take the test, despite the possibility of having a retarded child. When I thought about it, I was surprised at myself for graciously accepting this possibility; this is not common for most Asians. If I had not been influenced by American culture, I would have had the amniocentesis and possibly had an abortion if the results were negative. I would not have had the courage to raise a child with a disability.

In Asia, the disabled are treated as less than fully human. Although some governments, such as Korea, have taken the lead in encouraging acceptance, the general public's treatment of people with disabilities leaves much to be desired. Mental retardation or physical disability is a stigma to a family, partly because of the influence of Buddhism. According to Buddhism, life is a series of causes and consequences, and a person's disability may be punishment for having behaved badly in a former life or for having a cruel ancestor. Thus, family members with mentally retarded children are often ashamed and rarely tell others about them. An elementary school classmate of mine in Korea had a handicapped brother. Whenever I visited her house, her mother put him in a bathroom or somewhere else where visitors couldn't see him. Thirty years later, public perception of disabilities in Asia has not improved much. Even in Japan, the most industrially advanced and urbanized society in Asia, disabled people face discrimination, humiliation, and inconvenience every day. In an article entitled "Japan's 'Unuseful People,'" an American reporter concluded that disabled Japanese are "second-class citizens in a first-class country." Since they are not considered ordinary people, they have a challenging time finding mates or jobs. Kenzaburo Oe, a Japanese author who won the Nobel Prize for literature, candidly shared his account of life with a handicapped son in his book *A Healing Family*. He commented:

> I have come to know many disabled people,
> their families, and those who help with
> their rehabilitation, and I have seen how
> each shoulders his or her own burdens. The
> signs of this suffering are clearly visible on
> the faces of the handicapped, even when
> they have reached the stage of acceptance;
> and those around are no doubt similarly
> marked.[5]

Americans' openness to other issues, such as adoption, is also admirable. Unfortunately, Asians' view of adoption is similar to their view of disabilities. In Asia, adoptions occur only within the family; if a man doesn't have a child, his brother may give him his own son or daughter to adopt. Confucian ancestor worship generated an overpowering sense of family lineage and a strong emphasis on biological relationships. When a Japanese couple had a daughter but no son, they adopted a boy who would marry their daughter and assume their surname. Not surprisingly, Asians are amazed when American families are willing to adopt children with no blood relation. They are even more bewildered when American couples enthusiastically adopt children with disabilities or serious handicaps. In Hong Kong even children with birthmarks are avoided by adoptive parents because the Chinese associate them with bad luck. In contrast, Americans strive to accept others as they are—light- or dark-skinned, fat or skinny, tall or short, perfect or imperfect. Although there is certainly room for improve-ment in the system, Americans are more accepting and open than almost any other group. Americans believe in the worth of every human soul and are committed to allowing all people to exercise their potential, regardless of their background or their mental or physical condition.

As educator John Gardner commented, "The release of human potential, the release of individual dignity, and the liberation of human spirit—these are the deepest and truest goals of the hearts and minds of the American people."

Openness and Friendliness

Two male college students had just arrived in the United States. One was from Germany, and the other was from Japan. As they were sitting and chatting on a campus lawn, an American female student passed by and said "Hi" with a friendly smile. The German student thought that this was unnatural, and the Japanese student jumped to his feet and asked the girl for her telephone number. Like these stu-dents, visitors from other countries often wonder why American strangers say hello to them on the street or nod to them in the elevator.

Americans are some of the friendliest people in the world. You might meet some unfriendly faces in large metropolitan areas, but you can expect to hear greetings or see smiles in most places. Having become accustomed to such friendliness in America, I feel unwelcome when I go to Asia, even to my home country. A few years ago, I attended a breakfast meeting in Korea. The participants were mostly business and civic leaders in Seoul. I sat at a table with nine other people, all of us strangers. There was complete silence at the table. All ten of us were reading the meeting agenda and eating breakfast. Finally, an emcee asked the participants to introduce themselves. Only then did we hesitantly greet one another.

Living in a land of immigrants, Americans have generally been open to newcomers. At the start of the 1998 baseball season, 21 percent of the players on major league rosters were born outside of the continental United States. This statistic also reflects America's merit-based culture. Americans are willing to accept anyone who can add value to the nation. One night, David Letterman presented "the top 10 signs that the New York Yankees are getting arrogant." According to the list, number one was "Sometimes they let an American guy pitch." While Letterman made fun of the Yankees' diversity, a Japanese author, Ayako Sato, challenged the Japanese to learn from American baseball fans. In her book *The Art of Self-Expression for the Internationalist*, Sato argued that the Japanese should learn American openness toward foreign players and acceptance of them. She reminded readers that Japanese sumo fans had rejected a Hawaiian-born Japanese American sumo champion simply because he was not a native-born Japanese.

Asians are polite to ingroup members, whom they consider themselves related to, but they can be indifferent to outsiders. This trait allows them to be rude in public places, such as at ball games or on subways, because they are dealing with people they don't know. Even with potential customers, most Asians (outside of Japan and Thailand) do not smile. Some salesclerks in Asia don't even ask, "May I help you?" In fact, for the 1994 International Women's

Conference, the Chinese government had to issue a special ban on some common rude responses. The banned phrases included "Go ask somebody else," "If you think the bus is slow, get off," "I don't care who you tell," "Don't ask if you won't buy," "I don't have change; go find some yourself," and "Get to the back of the line." For the 1988 Olympics in Seoul, Koreans had a nationwide smile campaign to make the foreign visitors feel welcome. Even in such a polite society as Japan, companies have hired trainers to teach employees to practice smiling by putting chopsticks between their upper and lower teeth. I believe that the success of McDonald's in Asia may be due in part to friendliness. The smiles of their employees, who are trained by McDonald's University, must charm Asian customers, who aren't used to such friendliness.

Americans also show their friendliness by including people in activities. They are glad to share the fun with others, even if they don't know them well. Many American friends have invited me to meetings, parties, or games as their guest, and I have always felt welcomed, even if I did not know the host or hostess. People always say, "The more, the merrier." Americans also exhibit their friendliness by complimenting the people they meet. Many Americans initiate conversations with strangers by offering compliments such as "Nice outfit" or "I like your earrings." One American friend told me one of her grandmother's favorite sayings: "If you don't have something nice to say, don't say anything at all." Praise or positive feedback costs nothing, and it creates and helps to maintain goodwill.

It is true that America has its share of moody and unfriendly people. And not everyone's smile or compliment is sincere. A Ukrainian immigrant told me about an experience she had when she first arrived in the United States. When an American co-worker asked, "How are you?" she was prepared to have an actual conversation, and she felt humiliated when the co-worker quickly walked away. Wanting to make friends in her new country, she had rehearsed what she was going to say. With her limited English, she had to think in Ukrainian and then translate her thoughts into English. She didn't realize that in America, a "Hi" can stand alone. Thus, newcomers commonly express their frustration over what they perceive to be Americans' superficial friendliness. Others find American friendliness too intense. An overzealous handshake or pat on the back makes some non-Americans feel uncomfortable.

Nevertheless, America is one of the most pleasant and upbeat places in the world. During President Clinton's inaugural ceremony, Maya Angelou read, "Say simply, very simply, with hope...'Good morning.'" As more Americans do so with a genuine wish for others' happiness, and learn to do so consistently, America will become an even friendlier place.

Pursuit of Fun

For Americans, the pursuit of happiness is serious business. "The happiest place on the earth" is a slogan posted all over Disneyland, the symbol of America for many people around the world. Countless bars in America feature a "happy hour" during which people are invited to have a good time while enjoying complimentary hors d'oeuvres and discounted drinks. McDonald's restaurants serve "Happy Meals" for children, which include collectible toys and keep them coming back for more. In contrast, happiness is not a part of the daily language of ordinary Asians. When researchers asked people in India and China about happiness, the most common answer was, "We have never thought about that." People rarely ask each other, "Are you happy?"

Americans may not be happy all the time, but they still want to have fun. Americans love to party, and almost any reason will do: neighborhood block party, beach party, Super Bowl party, slumber party, bachelor party, going-away party, Oscar-night party, tornado survival party, Y2K party, and many more. There are also many traditional holiday parties: Valentine's Day, St. Patrick's Day, Easter, Memorial Day, the Fourth of July, Labor Day, Halloween, Thanksgiving, Christmas, and New Year's Eve. Americans search for reasons to have a party: finished a paper? won a game? filed your tax return? paid off your mortgage? Even for many of those who aren't "party animals," parties are a part of their lives. College libraries and dormitories are completely vacated on Friday and Saturday nights. Indeed, Americans like to make ordinary life experiences fun. Even a going-away party, retirement party, or baby shower usually involves more than just getting together and giving gifts; it often has a theme or a surprise element.

In contrast, having fun or being creative is not always easy in Asia. Some might argue that, until recently, Asians couldn't afford to have fun because life was too hard. Many people were poor and politically or socially oppressed. In fact, in China and Korea, an everyday greeting was "Did you eat?" rather than "How are you?" If a person had eaten, that meant that he or she was okay. Although many Asians don't have to worry about their livelihood anymore, they don't seem to have the spontaneity that Americans delight in. As their countries become more affluent, though, Asians are seeking happiness and having more fun. The most common Asian way of having fun is drinking and doing karaoke. Other fun activities include video games and gambling. There is no surprise or theme, however. Furthermore, parties are often reserved for ingroup members. Parties that are open to everybody, like many of those in America, are difficult to pull off and rare in Asia, because people are wary of those with whom they are not acquainted.

Americans not only love fun activities; they also love to laugh. Comics pervade the Sunday papers, late-night television comedians compete head-to-head, and sitcoms crowd prime time. Americans' dedication to fun extends to all aspects of their lives, from politics to management. American speeches are peppered with jokes, whereas Asian speeches are often filled with apologies. In Asia, authority figures are not supposed to kid around. Once I asked a scholar in Eastern philosophy why Asian leaders do not joke in public. He answered, "Asians expect their leaders to be leaders, not comedians or clowns." In fact, in old China, actors used to occupy the bottom notch of the social scale, in spite of the popularity of theater. In contrast, most Americans—leaders and followers alike—must have a good dose of humor on a daily basis. Whether on greeting cards or calendars, coffee mugs or wall plaques, they want something funny. Comic strips are posted on office doors and walls. Top managers get management lessons and employees get laughs from comics such as *Dilbert*. Many Americans find room for humor everywhere.

Thus, America's domination of the entertainment industry is not an accident. Because of Americans' earnest desire to have fun, the U.S. entertainment industry has grown by leaps and bounds. Japanese film producers complain that the Japanese perceive all movies to be American-made. When I took my son to a children's theme park in Australia, I found its stores filled with Barney, Pooh, and Mickey Mouse dolls and gifts. American movies are shown from Bangkok to Rome as soon as they are released. On French television I saw *Friends*, *M*A*S*H*, and many other American programs. American music is played abroad as soon as it hits the *Billboard* charts. Fun-loving Americans even believe that learning should be fun to be effective. Americans want to learn interactively, whereas Asians want to learn passively, by listening to lectures. Recently, when I attended a half-day seminar, the instructor listed a few ground rules for the class, one of which was to have fun. Even the defensive driving classes for ticketed drivers have humor built in. It must have been an American who first thought of the term *edutainment* (educational entertainment).

Of course, there is an excessive side to the American obsession with fun. Recently I read an article in *Family Fun* magazine titled "It's Moving Day: 16 Ways to Pack It with Fun." One of the sixteen suggestions was to send a letter to your new home addressed to yourself. The writer added, "When we arrived at our new home in Connecticut, we were greeted by a letter in our mailbox from some friendly well-wishers—us." I fail to see how anyone can have fun by adding one more task (writing a letter) to the mayhem of packing and moving. Americans who are obsessed with having fun sometimes set unrealistic expectations for themselves and then get caught up in planning to have fun. I know a mother who works over fifty hours a week. She told me about three parties she had organized for her son's third birthday. One was at his day-care center. Since her son's passion was fire engines, she baked a cake with a fire engine on it and arranged for a local firefighter to show up at the party. Another was a formal sit-down dinner for family members. When she was growing up, her mother had given formal dinner parties on the children's birthdays, so she wanted to continue the tradition. The third party was for her son's friends in the neighborhood. She was already overworked without these parties. When I asked her how she could do so much, she told me, "My husband says that I do it until I collapse."

As long as they do not overdo it, I appreciate Americans' fun-loving spirit, which is hard to find in Asia. Life is a serious business, but humor and fun help us keep going. Even in tragic situations, humor can bring out the best in us. By laughing with others and at ourselves, we can redirect our energy from negative to positive. Some argue that Americans developed the habit of having fun because they were taught to "rejoice and be glad" by early Christians. Others claim that wealth and comfortable lifestyles have encouraged Americans to look for ways to enjoy life and leisure. Whatever its origin, I am having fun in America.

Turning Scars into Stars

Although coping with pain is not a typical strength of Americans, many Americans have graciously turned their misfortunes into opportunities to serve others. MADD (Mothers Against Drunk Drivers) was started in 1980 by a mother who had lost her thirteen-year-old daughter in an accident involving a drunk driver. With a mission to stop drunk driving and to support its victims, MADD now has more than 550 chapters and community action teams around the country. Jim Brady, press secretary to former president Ronald Reagan, was permanently paralyzed in an assassination attempt on the president. During his recuperation, he and his wife initiated the Brady bill, which makes buying guns in America more difficult. Christopher Reeve, the *Superman* star who was paralyzed after a fall from a horse, has committed himself to supporting research into spinal cord injuries. An actress who lost her sister to cancer created a foundation that provides cancer patients and their families with emotional and spiritual support.

The list of ordinary Americans who have turned their personal tragedies into public triumphs is a long one. When a seven-year-old American boy, Nicholas Green, was shot to death in Italy in 1994, his parents donated his organs to Italian children. This gesture of love made Italians do some soul-searching and raised their awareness about organ donation. When two young men (Juan Cotera and Brandon Shaw) were kidnapped and drowned in Austin, Texas, by two teenagers, their parents turned their energies toward stopping juvenile violence. They formed the Shaw Cotera Juvenile Violence Consortium. By combining their efforts with those of policy makers, university researchers, and families of crime victims, they have made significant progress toward implementing prevention programs that work. Sarah Buel, a Harvard Law School graduate and a former battered wife, teaches a class on domestic violence. She inspires other abused women to get out of their situations and pursue their dreams.

Even famous Americans are committed to educating the public or helping others. Unlike most famous Asians, who are concerned about their public images and keep personal challenges a secret, American celebrities and public figures are willing to share their anguish and redemption if they can see the benefit of that sharing. Betty Ford, the former first lady, admitted her addiction to alcohol and founded the Betty Ford Clinic. Former governor of Texas Ann Richards is open about her addiction to alcohol and regularly speaks at Alcoholics Anonymous conventions. Oprah Winfrey frequently talks about her rape by a family member. Kathy Cronkite, the daughter of former CBS news anchor Walter Cronkite, wrote about her depression to help people understand the disease. In her book, other celebrities also speak about their bouts with depression. Americans' openness about their problems helps reassure those who face similar challenges that they are not alone and that there is light at the end of the tunnel.

Many of the problems that Americans face also exist in Asia, but they are not dealt with as openly, nor do Asians turn their scars into stars—that is, use their personal pain to help others. Maybe the tradition of fatalism has provided Asians with a different coping mechanism. They learn to accept their challenges and assume that others will do the same, so they do not feel the need to create support systems. Besides, Asian history is filled with wars and tragedies; Asians accept their suffering as a way of life. Another explanation for why Asians do not share their tragedies openly is their desire to save face. Face is a concept that all Asians are familiar with;

it is one's reputation in a group or community. Admitting a problem might result in losing face. Thus, most people keep their problems to themselves. Asians are less likely to see mental health professionals, and rape victims often fail to report their attacks for fear of being ostracized. Rapes by acquaintances are rarely prosecuted and are often viewed with a "she asked for it" attitude. Sometimes husbands of rape victims leave their wives, perceiving them as "damaged." Nor is the problem of sexual harassment taken seriously. In many Asian organizations, women rarely press charges against men who sexually harass them. In a male-dominated culture in which men have written the rules, men are not punished for their aggressions, and women pay the price. Rather than having compassion for victims and helping them recover, Asian society punishes them.

Incest and domestic violence are also swept under the rug; they are treated as family affairs. Traditionally, women and children were men's property and without social status. The traditional attitude toward a married woman is expressed in *The Great Learning for Women*, written by Japanese author Kaibara Ekken: "The husband is Heaven to the wife. Disobeying Heaven only incurs righteous punishment." Given this attitude, even close family members and friends secretly believe that the victim of family violence deserves the abuse. Due to these secret "family affairs," scars remain for a long time, and people remain lonely and wounded in silence.

It is the belief that every cloud has a silver lining that makes Americans so open about their personal tragedies. Americans understand that we are all human and therefore fallible. Thus, one failure or problem or tragedy in life is not the end of the world. When Americans make mistakes, most of them can forgive themselves and bounce back. They try not to wallow in their misfortunes. Americans give themselves and others a second chance, a third chance, a fourth chance—until they make it on their own.

Being Practical

Americans have raised practicality almost to an art form. For example, Americans typically ask people to bring food or drinks to parties they are hosting. It is not uncommon for party invitations to state "BYOB" (bring your own beer [or bottle]) or "BYOF" (bring your own food) or "potluck." Many Americans ask for doggy bags at restaurants and take home their uneaten food to eat later. They expect to pay individually when they eat at a group outing. They are not ashamed to use a discount coupon at a restaurant. When they invite guests for dinner, they prepare a simple meal with an entree, salad, vegetable dish, and dessert.

These customs are not as common in Asia. People are afraid to ask their guests to bring something because they will be considered cheap. And they cannot serve just a few simple dishes, because there is a certain expectation of the host. When Asians eat out, they don't ask for doggy bags, even if more than half their portion is left over. When they go out as a group, many people pay for others (often reluctantly) in order not to lose face.

Americans are also practical in gift giving. They do not give gifts nearly as often as the Japanese or Koreans do. The Japanese and Koreans give gifts all the time, creating an obligation to return the favor; it is a continuous ritual.

Anthropologist Harumi Befu counted at least thirty-five different terms for gifts in Japan, ranging from an "introductory goodwill gift" to "funerary gifts." Even at weddings, grooms and brides are supposed to give "return gifts" to guests, in addition to hosting costly receptions. The families of the bride and groom also exchange gifts. The bride's family, especially, is expected to send expensive gifts to the groom's parents, brothers and sisters, and other significant relatives. The value of gifts is the talk of relatives and friends for a long time. Going overboard, some parents put themselves deeply in debt to pay for the weddings of their children. In fact, my parents had four daughters, and their friends joked that by the time they paid for the weddings of all four, all they would have left in their possession would be underwear!

Americans exchange gifts, but their gifts tend to be within their budgets. Holiday gifts of money to nonprofit organizations and charities on behalf of a second party are popular. Americans appreciate the thought behind the gift; its monetary value is secondary. A beautiful rose or a homemade cake warms the receiver's heart. It's much sweeter to send a gift from the heart than to send one out of obligation. In contrast, Asians feel obligated to buy big gifts for others because money talks, not one's heart. As a result, in giving, they torment their souls instead of liberating them. Gift giving becomes an ordeal.

Americans also demonstrate their practicality in their attire. The informal dress code that Microsoft and Apple Computer initiated has set a new standard for other high-tech companies and, to some extent, for all of corporate America. Casual Fridays have become common at many American corporations, which have found that dressing down improves creativity and employee morale. It is not uncommon for professional women in big cities to wear sneakers, instead of high heels, until they get to the office, because they often have to walk quite a distance from the bus or subway. They don't worry about others looking at them or passing judgment. Americans prefer comfortable clothes on outings—T-shirts and shorts or jeans.

Being practical, Americans are not ashamed of giving or buying used items. My first American roommate asked me whether I wanted to use her slip, which didn't fit her anymore. At the time, I thought it was strange to offer used clothing, but later, I realized that this was the American way. Even celebrities contribute to consignment stores. The late Jacqueline Kennedy Onassis reportedly sold her clothes this way. One popular store, Star Wares in Los Angeles, offers slightly used clothing from famous movie stars, who donate the proceeds to their favorite charities. Cher and Elizabeth Taylor are two of the many celebrities who participate in this American phenomenon.

Visiting secondhand stores, thrift shops, garage sales, and flea markets has been an eye-opening experience for someone like me, who thought that buying secondhand was only for the poor. It is true that one man's trash is another man's treasure in America. "Previously loved" items are in demand in all categories, from baby furniture to used cars to old pianos. Even affluent people buy one- to two-year-old cars to minimize depreciation. People search for good deals at garage sales or in weeklies that specialize in secondhand listings. Garage sales can be used to teach children about getting a good deal. When I had my garage sale, a little boy came and bought a silk necktie for his father's birthday.

In Asia, exchanging used items is done within the family, but not outside. Like so many American practices, however, the secondhand market concept is being exported to Asia. In Korea, green sheets (classified ads for inexpensive items) are now being published, and the *byeo-rook-si-jang* (flea market) is thriving. In Japan, consignment stores have started opening up, often accepting clothing and accessories only from flight attendants, who frequently travel overseas and buy the latest name-brand fashions.

One Asian practice that Americans observe, though to a lesser degree, is the custom of giving money as a gift. Asians give cash gifts for birthdays, holidays, weddings, and funerals. The practice is meant to divide the expense for such special occasions among family and friends. The gift givers know that they will be "reimbursed" in their own time of need. By giving and receiving cash, Americans could also save the time and energy spent buying and returning unwanted gifts or putting on garage sales. Everybody can use cash.

Sharing Romantic Feelings

Although author John Gray claims that men are from Mars and women are from Venus, American couples communicate their feelings more expressively and romantically than their Asian counterparts do. Americans are very creative in letting their loved ones know about their feelings. From courtship to marriage, American men and women find 1,001 ways to say I love you to their significant others every day. Electronic and paper cards, flowers, balloons, teddy bears, chocolates, cookies, and cakes are only a few examples of how Americans send messages of love. Husbands and wives agonize over how to throw a memorable birthday party or find the perfect anniversary gift—the more unexpected, the better. To keep their romance alive, some couples use weekly dates, movie nights, candlelight dinners, weekend getaways, cruises and trips, and so on. Even when they reach retirement age, many still exchange love notes or walk hand in hand.

In Asian literature, there are beautiful love stories, but lovers in real life rarely express their affection. Asian women often complain that their men are hopelessly unromantic. It is not that Asian women want to be pampered all the time, but a simple "I love you" is barely said once a courtship becomes a marriage. Most Asian men rarely say thank you to their wives, believing that doing so too often degrades the value of appreciation.

Married Asian women are not particularly romantic either. An American jeweler revealed this story about an Asian client: A Japanese man ordered a huge diamond ring for his wife. The ring was so expensive that the jeweler decided to deliver it in person. After the husband received the ring, he gave it to his wife with a smug look of pride on his face while the jeweler looked on. She tried the ring on, then left the room with an emotionless bow. Maybe the couple was shy because of an outsider's presence, but the American jeweler was stunned. If such a present had been given to an American woman, she would have been ecstatic with joy and gratitude.

In traditional Asia, many generations lived under one roof, so showing romantic feelings was difficult because there was no privacy. A Japanese woman wrote, "The rooms were not locked and usually the sliding doors that separated the rooms were kept open even on cold winter days, so my husband and I behaved like strangers to each other while we lived in the midst of watching eyes. It was a life in which individuality was completely killed in order to create harmony for the family." In such an environment, displays of affection were disrespectful to elders. Many Asians now have nuclear families, but the tradition of unromantic marriage continues.

Asian women complain that Asian men rarely remember their birthdays or anniversaries, and if they do remember, they tend not to do anything special. Somehow, Asian men perceive romantic or sentimental things as being effeminate. They rarely think to send cards or notes, much less surprise gifts. I can count on my American husband's creative ways of expressing his love for me. Sometimes he leaves me a note in my shoe or puts chocolate in my cosmetics bag. When he has to leave early for work, he cuts a piece of watermelon so that I can have an afternoon snack. Once when I returned from a business trip, I found all my nightgowns washed, pressed, and hung on hangers in the closet. Being Asian, I don't need the assurance of his love for me every day, but I certainly enjoy these simple acts of kindness, and I know they make him feel good about himself.

I rarely hear such things from Asian friends who are married to Asian men. When wives complain that their husbands never bring them flowers, the husbands commonly answer, "You have all my money. If you want some, why don't you buy them for yourself?" Many Asian men feel that real men should not show their feelings. A Korean friend of mine told me about her husband, who has lived in the United States for more than thirty years, since high school. One day, a businessman from Japan visited him, and it happened to be Valentine's Day. When they arrived at the restaurant for dinner that night, he was shocked to see that he and his Japanese guest were the only two men dining together.

Traditionally, Asian people suppressed their emotions because showing emotion was considered immature. Besides, Asians believed that if a man talked a lot, he was useless. A man was supposed to keep his feelings and thoughts inside. Those in the younger generation are getting better at expressing their feelings, but many are still shy about tender gestures of love. Interestingly, one of the most popular items that Japanese men buy on the Internet is flowers. When I asked the reason, a Japanese e-commerce executive answered, "The buyers don't feel embarrassed to buy flowers because they don't show their face or have to carry them." In the United States, in contrast, it is common to see a man carrying a bouquet of flowers either on the street or at an airport gate to give to his loved one.

Young people may be showing more affection in public and observing occasions like Valentine's Day by sending chocolates or flowers to their sweethearts, but some men still hold traditional male chauvinist attitudes. One Japanese student had to take her boyfriend out on Valentine's Day because he demanded that she show *her* love for *him*. Asian men defend themselves by saying that they love their wives in a deeper way than superficial Americans. But I want to know what is wrong with buying flowers and giving surprise gifts to their wives from time to time? Such simple, thoughtful gestures by my husband help me bear the more challenging days with him and be more patient with him when the less gentle side of him appears.

Indeed, the beauty of any relationship is to bring out the best in each other. Simple gestures can inspire our loved ones to be the best they can be. Asian couples accept marriage as a mundane institution with real-life issues to deal with, but it does not have to be so drab. It is important for couples to nurture their relationship in special ways. Of course, there is a downside to overemphasizing romance. Some Americans expect the romantic intensity of their relationships to continue after marriage or children. So they think that there is something wrong with their relationship if the flame dies down. Most Asians start with low expectations and are less likely to be disappointed.

Remaining Active throughout Life

"It's getting better and better every day," sang Liz Carpenter, a Texas writer in her eighties, along with her elderly friends in a television version of *New Passages*, a book written by Gail Sheehy. (Sheehy had to rewrite her original book, *Passages*, to take into account the vigorous elderly in America.) According to *New Passages*, the age of fifty is what forty used to be, and sixty is what fifty used to be. Although America is criticized for its youth-oriented culture, American elders enjoy more productive lives than their Asian counterparts do. From working as independent consultants to serving as volunteers, American elders can retain their zest for life. Comedian George Burns performed at Caesar's

Palace in Las Vegas for his ninety-eighth birthday. The late James Michener attended a network publishing workshop at the age of eighty-seven. Former president George Bush went skydiving in his seventies. Mike Wallace, now in his eighties, still does serious investigative reporting for CBS's *60 Minutes*.

It's not just a few celebrities who are actively engaged in lifelong learning and working. When I went to a lecture on American culture by Daniel Bell of the Library of Congress a few years ago, I was pleasantly surprised to find that most members of the audience were elderly. College enrollment for people over sixty-five went up 27 percent between 1991 and 1996. An eighty-five-year-old man in Florida enrolled in law school at Nova Southeastern University. A woman in her seventies told me that she was taking Spanish lessons. She did not know whether she would ever get to travel to Spain or Latin America, but she said, "You've got to use your brain to stay alert." My friend Jane, who received her Ph.D. at age sixty, is serving on the boards of several volunteer organizations, visited China as a U.S. representative for issues involving the elderly, and went to Scotland on an elder hosteling trip to celebrate her seventieth birthday.

According to the American Association of Retired Persons (AARP), the nation's largest organization of senior citizens, there are more than two million computer users among its thirty-three million members. They use their computers to monitor their investments, track their genealogy, document their recollections, and so on. Instructors say that senior citizens learn to use computers as fast as teenagers, once they master the mouse. Given this sizable elderly population that is eager to pursue lifelong learning, there are many opportunities for community organizations and others to offer classes for them.

In contrast, many Asian elderly expect to stop learning at a certain age. It is rare to see an elderly person visiting a library unless he or she was a scholar. The typical mentality for Asians over fifty-five is, "I'm old, so what is learning for?" or "I'm just going to travel a little and go away [die]." Opportunities for elders to lead productive lives or use their energy in positive ways are limited in Asia. Unlike in America, it is difficult in Asia for senior citizens to get jobs at restaurants, grocery stores, or elsewhere. In Asia, even the volunteer organizations do not appreciate the services of elders. In the United States, an eighty-year-old man who opens the door for patients at a hospital is one of almost 445,000 retired seniors who do volunteer work. They serve their community as public park guides, library storytellers, and literacy mentors, among many other roles.

Despite the myth that Asian elders enjoy respect from youth, such respect has never been an automatic right. Rather, elders have to earn respect for their wisdom. The long-held Confucian custom whereby the first son of each family cares for the parents is changing, and Asian elderly feel more lonely and isolated. Although many elderly still live with their children, they are bored with life and wonder how to spend each day.

In a society where seniors are expected to lead active lives, many American elderly learn to age with grace. I once read a list of gifts for older parents that an elderly woman had written for a local paper. It included cosmetics, perfumes, and accessories. Yes, my American husband's grandmother loved them. She lived to see ninety and delighted in being well dressed and well groomed at home or when visiting others. It feels good to see a grandmotherly woman who cares about her looks and knows how to present herself. Former bishop of New York Fulton J. Sheen was quoted as saying, "There are three ages of a man: youth, middle age, and 'my but you look good.'" Many American elderly look good indeed. In Asian countries, some elders tend to lose their social graces, regressing to untidy clothing, loose talk, and few table manners. They seem to think that their age excuses their poor etiquette. Contrasting the Asian elderly lifestyle with the American, one sees the difference between growing old and aging with grace.

Respect for Children's Voices

Once I called my neighbor to ask if I could hire her sixteen-year-old son to cut my grass. She said, "I'll ask him." If I had called an Asian mother, she might have said, "I'll send him." Notwithstanding cases of child abuse, Americans see children as independent beings. Despite the use of such universal parenting phrases as "Not under my roof," American parents give much more respect to their children than do parents in many other countries. Some American adults may have sad childhood memories of their parents' put-downs, but the fact is that many educated Asian parents aspire to model themselves after American parents in respecting their children's opinions and fostering their ability to express their ideas.

Most Americans listen to their children's views. A few years ago, Nike published the "Kids' Bill of Rights," which included the right to have a voice. When children exercise their rights, adults pay attention to them. Their voices are heard in families, churches, and the larger community. Children can take their causes to the public. When former Speaker of the House Newt Gingrich was ten, he was given an opportunity to present a proposal in front of the Harrisburg City Council in Pennsylvania. Being an animal lover, he thought the city should have a zoo and approached the person in charge. He was not dismissed as a kid who liked animals; on the contrary, the council actively listened to him. Thus, at a young age, Gingrich was able to test his aptitude for politics.

As a high school freshman in Florida, Dave Levitt saw that there was too much waste at his school cafeteria and convinced the administrators that uneaten food should go to the poor rather than to the dump. He then took his idea to the school board, which agreed to donate leftovers from ninety-two county schools. Now, as an adult, he and his sister are lobbying the state legislature to adopt a similar program statewide. His Operation Food for Thought has generated nearly ninety-five tons of food for the hungry.

American children are also given an earlier chance to express themselves in various fields than are Asian children. Universities offer summer camps for children with special talents: music, computer literacy, astronomy, baseball, leadership—you name it. Elementary and high schools have programs for gifted children; many programs are designed to nurture accelerated development in those with distinctive talents and brainpower. Leaders in various fields also make efforts to ensure that young talent is discovered and developed at an early age. Internships for high school students are available at corporations and government offices. When American children show talent, they are taken seriously, and age is not an obstacle.

Children are included in many other ways as well. When I travel across America, I'm impressed with the programs and materials available for children. For example, at Denali National Park in Alaska, the park rangers acknowledged my then three-year-old son as a junior ranger. I believe that many other national parks have similar programs. At state parks, museums, and galleries, parents can easily find interesting materials for their children. At the John F. Kennedy Library in Boston, I found a book on how to become a president. It was designed for young children and included chapters on how to select a campaign theme and how to write a speech. At restaurants, children often get paper and crayons to occupy them while they wait for their dinner. Americans may take these things for granted, but they show a regard for children—as well as keeping them too busy to get into trouble.

In contrast, children in Asia are not seen as people who have their own views or who have any right to express them. They are often left out of family conversations and decisions about their own lives. It's unusual for Asian parents to let their children choose their church, as the Clintons allowed their daughter Chelsea to do when she was only seven. Although young Asian couples tend to shower their children with material things, many parents still hold on to the traditionally authoritarian parenting style when it comes to children's choices and opinions. In China, where only one child is allowed per family, young children are spoiled as if they were the emperor's son, and their grandparents shower them with gifts. Nevertheless, in most Asian countries, parents are not that generous in granting children rights or privacy. Adults routinely regulate children's personal choices. Although there is merit to continuous supervision and strict regulations, Asian children are often shy about expressing their ideas. Now, thanks in part to the Internet, more and more children and teenagers are expressing their ideas and exchanging opinions freely (as much as governments allow).

Unaccustomed to making their own choices and decisions, Asian children often reluctantly let their parents make decisions for them. Some of them are tormented by the conflict between the desires of their parents and their own preferences. They may go to law school or medical school because their parents want them to, but they express their unhappiness. Sometimes, they still accept the spouses their parents choose, even if they are not satisfied with them. They do not have the courage to say no to their parents. Fortunately, Asian parents are starting to realize that they cannot always impose their wishes on their children, but there are still die-hard authoritarian parents who want to micromanage the lives of the young.

It is critical for a society to listen to children's voices to ensure their well-being. Whenever I hear about child abuse cases in the United States, I wonder what would happen if the same kinds of laws were adopted in Asia. Chin-Ning Chu, best-selling author of *The Asian Mind Game,* writes: "In five thousand years of Chinese history, there has been no concept of child abuse.... Under this concept, anything the parents can possibly do to the child is said to be for the child's own good." Incest has been suspected in Asia, but nobody knows how many are affected. Talking about it is almost taboo, because the family is the most important unit. Regardless of what happens inside the home, the family's first priority is to preserve continuity and maintain its reputation in the community. And Asian children shut down their emotions and suffer lifelong scars as a consequence.

Exposing Children to the Work Ethic

One Saturday morning I went to a picnic at a big ranch outside Austin, Texas. When I wanted to ride a paddleboat in a little pond, two young attendants were eager to help my family and other customers. Impressed with their professionalism, I asked one what grade he was in. He told me that he was a high school freshman; in fact, most of the ranch staff were high school students, and the whole place ran very smoothly. Young people in America begin learning the importance of work from an early age. They not only help around the house but also take such paid jobs as baby-sitting, lawn mowing, housecleaning, working at restaurants, or doing summer internships. Even in affluent families, children take part-time jobs for granted and do not complain about it; for example, a doctor's son may work at a hotel as a doorman, or an executive's daughter may be a cashier at a grocery store. It is common for high school students to work for pay during the summer, and many do community service without pay.

Many schools and communities have programs to expose young children to real-life experiences. In an elementary school in New York, children run kids' cafés through an entrepreneurial program. They conduct market research, set prices, and decide what items to feature on the menu. Young people with impressive computer skills are hired as contractors by computer shops to complete sophisticated programming assignments. Children are hired to serve as consultants to toy companies or video-game developers, and they are taken seriously for their ability to contribute to the business world.

In Asia, children work only if absolutely necessary or if their relatives have a family business. It is rare for well-dressed children to sell cookies or lemonade in front of stores or homes. I was a Girl Scout myself and never sold a cookie. When we needed funding for special events, we just asked our parents. So what is the social price for this attitude? "The father makes the money," goes the Cantonese proverb, "while the son spends it."

Through early work experiences, American youth learn the value of self-reliance, gain an understanding of people from different backgrounds, test their entrepreneurial talent, and even become rich. Bill Gates, former CEO of Microsoft and one of the richest men in the world, was paid to do computer programming at his high school and at several corporations when he was a teen. Warren Buffet, another wealthy American, set up a stand on the sidewalk in front of his family's Omaha house and sold gum to passersby in his first entrepreneurial project as a child. Then he sold lemonade—not on the quiet street where he lived, but in front of a friend's corner house, where the traffic was heavier. Michael Dell, CEO of Dell Computer Corporation, hired his high school friends to copy the names and addresses of recent applicants for marriage licenses— people he identified as a target market for subscriptions to a local newspaper. He made $18,000 and was only seventeen. One year later, he dropped out of the University of

Texas and earned $80,000 per month running a business selling PC clones by mail order, the first in the country to do so. Age doesn't count when it comes to entrepreneurship.

Other rich Americans also started early. The U.S. Trust survey of the wealthiest 1 percent of Americans—those individuals earning $200,000 or more a year or with three million dollars or more in assets—found that on average, they had their first jobs at age ten, typically delivering newspapers or baby-sitting. They started full-time work at eighteen and became business owners at twenty-nine. Many of them did not do so out of necessity. Unlike Asian children from affluent families, they were encouraged early on to learn the value of hard work and independence.

Americans develop additional life and job skills through their involvement in do-it-yourself projects around the house. One Saturday morning in Stamford, Connecticut, I heard the sound of water splashing outside my friend's apartment window. A little boy, wearing rubber boots, was helping to wash his father's car. I went outside to ask the man how old his son was; he was only three. No wonder so many men and women in America are handy. When I joined a college cooperative housing program as a graduate student, I was amazed at how capable the American students were in managing the co-op. Their backgrounds were as diverse as the U.S. population; yet all participated in getting the co-op started and ran it like professionals. From budgeting to member recruiting, cooking to carpentry, pest control to remodeling, they did almost everything themselves. If a co-op were ever run in an Asian country, I'm sure it would not be as self-sufficient.

In many Asian countries, where elitism prevails, adolescents are not equipped to do much more than academic work. In traditional China and Korea, the only way for a person to move up the social ladder was through education. In Japan, under the feudal system, samurai valued physical strength, but education played a significant role in a person's life and career. Thus, Asian parents had to make certain that their children got into the right school and developed the right connections, because their careers were determined by academic achievement. Furthermore, according to the Confucian teaching of filial piety, children owed their bodies to their parents, so they had to avoid physical strain and exhaustion so as not to damage themselves. Even now, parents are anxious about their offspring wasting their energies and physically damaging themselves. Parents do not expect children to help with housework; they tell them to study instead.

Exposing their children to a variety of tasks helps them be better prepared for their jobs. When I compare twenty-two-year-old Asian employees with Americans of the same age, I see that the Americans act much more professionally. If American youth could improve their basic skills—reading, writing, and arithmetic—and learn to save money from their hard-earned income, America would continue to have one of the most competitive workforces in the world, blessed with multiple skills.

Volunteerism

America's third president, Thomas Jefferson, said that government is strongest when everyone feels a part of it. One way that Americans feel a part of things is through volunteer activities. With America boasting more than eighty million volunteers each year, I cannot imagine what a day would be like without them. There is no American whose life is not touched by volunteers. Dedicated volunteers work everywhere, from hospitals to national parks, from political campaigns to soup kitchens. With the mentality that "service is a rent everyone pays for living," Americans shape a better world around them.

Americans lead the world not only in the number of causes they serve as volunteers but also in their public support of volunteerism. Even famous Americans take their volunteer work seriously: Farm Aid spearheaded by Willie Nelson, the Muscular Dystrophy Association Telethon with Jerry Lewis, AIDS fund-raising by Elizabeth Taylor, the "Just Say No" campaign of Nancy Reagan, Feed the World with Quincy Jones, and many other memorable campaigns.

Volunteers in America are mobilized like pros. They know how to organize successful events and run community service organizations professionally. The Red Cross alone has nearly one and a half million volunteers, and Elizabeth Dole passed up her salary of two hundred thousand dollars the first year she was chairwoman to stress the importance of volunteerism. During the 1997–98 academic year, six hundred thousand college students provided twenty-nine million hours of service. If the U.S. government had to pay for all the things volunteers do, it would cost hundreds of billions of dollars annually.

In volunteer work, there is no class distinction. Title or status does not matter. Volunteers need only a willingness to serve and compassion for others. Former president Jimmy Carter is well known for his volunteer work with

Habitat for Humanity, which builds houses for low-income families. Kim Clark, dean of the Harvard Business School, served as a volunteer coach for a youth basketball team on weekends. Stephanie Crawford, a professor in Chicago, helps feed the homeless every Monday night. In their volunteer work, they forget about their career accomplishments. People with different backgrounds and education work together harmoniously to support whatever cause inspires them.

In volunteer work, just as there is no class distinction, there is no old or young. All work together to serve their community. Winners of the Jefferson Award, honoring ordinary people who contributed to their communities through volunteer work, ranged from a fourteen-year-old who taught English to new immigrant children to a woman of 106 who had volunteered more than 128,000 hours over the course of her life. Children learn the value of giving from an early age. A five-year-old boy who participates in a walk-a-thon to raise money for cancer research, a ten-year-old girl who sells cookies to raise funds for a local children's center, and elementary school students who work as docents at local art museums are examples of young volunteers.

In volunteer work, there is no cause that is too small. Any cause is good if it can improve people's environment or help others reach their potential. From domestic violence hot lines to MADD, volunteers raise public awareness of social ills and cures. From political events to literacy councils, they educate the public and get the community involved. From marathons to international hospitality groups, they encourage the community to stay healthy and friendly. From granting the wishes of dying children (Make-a-Wish

Foundation) to delivering meals to the elderly (Meals On Wheels), volunteers share the spirit of love and give the gift of hope.

Through volunteer work, Americans also guide the next generation. Many high achievers attribute their success to their mentors. The late tennis champion Arthur Ashe rated the importance of having a mentor an eleven on a scale of one to ten. Every year, three million men and women work as volunteer coaches, serving as mentors as well. Big Brother/ Big Sister programs are available in many cities, and professional organizations have mentoring programs for women and minorities. The Junior Achievement organizations have formed alliances between public schools and corporations to prepare the underprivileged for one-on-one work with mentors.

Volunteerism is becoming prevalent in corporate America as well. High-tech and pharmaceutical companies encourage students' interest in science through their employee volunteers. Through each network, the hard-earned wisdom and knowledge of elders are transferred, and over time, new leaders are born and mentored.

Americans take their volunteerism with them when they go abroad. IBM Korea started a program that matched underprivileged children with employees, an uncommon practice in Korean corporations. Many American expatriates' spouses organize community service activities or join volunteer service organizations. By being involved in their communities, they learn local customs and become involved in their new culture. Americans bloom where they are planted. In contrast, when Asians move to the United States, most do not get involved in community service. In the book *The Japan that Can Say No*, the authors criticized their countrymen abroad for sticking to Japanese communities. Asians may join their ethnic communities or churches, but rarely do they go out of their extended-family cocoons and contribute to or become involved in their new communities.

It is through their volunteer work that Americans build their community. From neighborhood-watch programs to environmental issues, they don't wait for the government to initiate action; they take action to bring about the changes they desire in their communities. In contrast, Asians are indifferent to issues outside their homes and families. In Singapore, as of the mid-1990s, only about one in ten people did volunteer work. Lee Kuan Yew, former prime minister of Singapore, admitted that his government had to take action on many social issues because people did not take the initiative to form grassroots movements. For Asians who are loyal to the Confucian tradition of valuing basic relationships, their foremost concern is to take care of the needs of their ingroups: family, church, school, and region of origin.

Of course, there is the question whether charity in America should begin at home. Dr. Rosabeth Moss Kanter, author of *World Class*, observed a correlation between fading American familism and volunteerism. She writes, "Americans who are not capable of building a meaningful relationship with a family member have a desperate need for connection outside their homes and actively participate in serving a cause to feel good." It is possible that if all Americans took care of their own family members and directed their compassion toward their families and immediate communities, there would be less need for government programs and less need for volunteers. Nevertheless, Asians have a lot to learn from Americans in valuing the volunteer spirit.

In the United States, grades are not the only factor in evaluating school applicants and job candidates. From Rhodes scholar selections to college applications, excellence in other areas such as leadership, volunteer activities, sports, and arts is equally important. The college entrance examination systems in Japan and Korea, known as "examination hell," emphasize grades so heavily that virtues such as community service or leadership are essentially ignored. Students spend most of their hours studying, leaving home as early as 4:30 A.M. for "cram schools" and coming home as late as midnight from after-school classes. In Japan, almost five million children—including one million in elementary school—attend some fifty thousand *juku*, privately operated cram schools. Chinese parents admit that the regimen is so intense that many eighteen-year-olds have little experience taking care of their own personal needs, much less the needs of others.

Gradually, Asians are starting to see the benefits of volunteerism. More and more people are getting to know the term *grassroots*. Corporations encourage executives to volunteer at orphanages. Schools encourage students to do volunteer work. Medical professionals have outreach programs. The Japanese have accepted volunteerism, but with a twist. In Japan, there is a "bank" for volunteers. Based on the volunteer hours they have worked (deposited), volunteers can receive a like amount of volunteer service when they need it. These are examples of positive changes, but Asia still needs to learn the benefit of serving a worthy cause that is larger than their own lives.

Generosity

When faced with any kind of disaster, people all over the world can rely on the generosity of Americans, who are always among the first to offer help—to Rwandan refugees, Bosnian war victims, Turkish earthquake survivors, Venezuelan flood victims, Chinese orphans, Russian homeless, and others. Americans have a natural tendency to rush to help people in adversity, and their generosity has brought tremendous benefits not only to their own country but also to the world.

It was during the latter part of the nineteenth century that great philanthropic organizations were formed in the United States by Americans who had accumulated large fortunes. Since then, Americans have given their time, money, and resources generously to promote various causes, whether a social agenda, medical research, or arts conservation. Americans have built long-lasting foundations, such as the United Way and Goodwill, to help people in need. Many medical research projects on breast cancer, Parkinson's disease, AIDS, and other ills are supported by Americans who want to help people become free from debilitating diseases. Often, people give to medical research because one of their family members is (or was) afflicted with a disease. Public television and classical music stations are funded by private donors.

It is obvious that the tax code to a certain extent has encouraged Americans to be generous. In the 1930s and after World War II, swiftly rising taxes and a steep inheritance tax exerted a significant influence on giving. But even before there were tax incentives, Americans gave to the causes they believed in. Even the colonists gave private funds to Harvard and Yale, hospitals, and other institutions, and in the nineteenth century, rich people wanted to donate their wealth to worthy causes to lessen the inequality of capitalism.

In giving, Americans have two great examples to follow: Andrew Carnegie and John D. Rockefeller. Carnegie's lifetime benefactions totaled about $350 million, and at the time of his death, Rockefeller had given various charities and endowments over $530 million. They have both become household names associated with philanthropy around the world. Some people have even attempted to outdo Carnegie and Rockefeller. George Soros, an immigrant from Hungary, has donated $650 million to various causes. Ted Turner has committed one billion dollars to the United Nations. Bill Gates is continuing the tradition in creating his own legacy. However, donors are not always upper-class citizens—even people who make under ten thousand dollars a year give what they can, sharing their blessings gladly.

Perhaps more important, Americans' generosity is not always materialistic. I have found that they are often generous in spirit as well. When I first came to America, I landed at Los Angeles International Airport. My friend could not meet me at the airport, and I was supposed to take a cab to her house. Since it was already dark, I was unsure whether taking a cab would be a good idea. I asked a couple I had just met whether they thought it was safe to take a taxi at night. Although they were at the airport to pick up their own friend, the couple offered to drive me to my destination and took two hours of their time to find my friend's house. When I asked them how I could return their kindness, they just told me, "Pass it on."

Since that initial positive experience on my first day in America, I have continually experienced Americans' generosity. When I had no place to stay between semesters in graduate school, various classmates invited me to stay at their homes. I never had to spend any holidays alone, thanks to my wonderful American friends, who treated me like a family member. Complete strangers also opened their homes and communities and afforded me a unique American experience. Through the church-sponsored International Students' Program, I spent wonderful two-week vacations with families in Jacksonville, Florida, and DeSoto, Texas, and experienced hospitality from entire communities. The host families were by no means among the richest or most educated Americans. They were ordinary people who believed in sharing their blessings. Their giving and sharing have left an indelible impression on me and inspired me to follow their example.

In Asia, help is usually available only among families and ingroups. The Confucian emphasis on basic human relationships contributed to a strict division between ingroups and outgroups. Often segregating "we" from "they," many Asians have closed their hearts to strangers. Their paternalism and openheartedness exist only for the people with whom they share particulars—family, school, company, region, and so on. Thus, in Asia, taking care of one's ingroup is the foremost concern, and outsiders' needs are not important.

Not surprisingly, many Asians are impressed with Americans' generosity toward strangers. They marvel at the compassion and humanitarianism that work such great wonders in many parts of the world. From Asia to Africa many schools and hospitals have been built by donations from Americans. And although Americans give their time and resources out of simple goodwill, their gifts contribute to producing a pro-American spirit around the world.

Embracing World Service

The majority of Americans believe that the United States has a special role to play in the world. Many Americans want to help the world overcome what John F. Kennedy called in his inaugural address the "common enemies of man: tyranny, poverty, disease, and war itself." Through the Peace Corps, a government service organization, nearly 140,000 dedicated Americans have given up the comfortable lifestyle of the U.S. to bring health and education to less-advantaged people around the world. Currently sixty-five hundred volunteers are working in ninety underdeveloped countries, proudly serving their country and sharing their skills and technology. From an agricultural specialist working in Tanzania to a doctor in a remote Thai village, Americans donate their skills and resources to enhance the quality of human life around the world.

Certainly, the American spirit of world service has inspired a few Asian countries. Korea now has its own version of the Peace Corps to serve less-developed countries. The Japanese have funded development programs in Asia, but some Japanese criticize their fellow citizens for their isolationist attitude.

If Americans cannot go abroad, they practice humanity at home. America has granted asylum to political prisoners and refugees from other countries. They have accepted

European Jews, Vietnamese, Cubans, Chinese, Russians, and countless others who were oppressed in their own countries. After the Vietnam War in 1975, 850,000 refugees entered the United States through special legislation; no Asian neighbors welcomed them. Even ordinary people participate in humanitarian causes. In 1956, Bertha Holt, an American housewife, began the Holt International Children's Services at the age of fifty. She herself adopted eight foreign babies and helped sixty thousand children get adopted through the organization. Thanks to caring Americans like Holt, children from Brazil, China, Korea, and Romania are finding new homes in America. Despite occasional anti-American outbursts, people around the world are grateful to Americans who have selflessly given and shared the blessings from their hearts.

Using their economic might, Americans work to prevent child labor in less-developed countries and fight for other civil liberties abroad. Many Europeans think that America's ideals are impractical and presumptuous. Indeed, Americans' overzealousness and self-righteousness have caused resentment in European and Asian countries alike. Some Asians criticize Americans for interfering in the affairs of other countries, as if they are somehow superior. Americans may be naive or presumptuous, preaching to the world about social justice and peace when there are huge domestic problems to be solved. Yet it is still noble to try to treat social ills by exporting American dreams and ideals to other countries.

One of America's biggest contributions to the world is its education of future world leaders. As of 2000, there were over 600,000 foreign students studying in the United States.

Fulbright scholarships and Rotary Clubs have sponsored scholars from all over the world, giving them the opportunity to do research and teach in America. Since the Fulbright Act was signed in 1946, providing for the exchange of students and teachers between America and other countries, 131,484 foreign scholars have benefited. The U.S. higher education system has already educated many world leaders and has indirectly influenced their ideologies and philosophies.

In the nineteenth century, young American scholars typically studied in Europe, especially in Germany. The flow of students seeking superior education was from America to Europe. The United States did not emerge as a major center for foreign studies until after World War II, when American higher education expanded rapidly and improved its quality dramatically. Since then, the U.S. has become a top host of international students, educating world leaders who have returned home and often changed the course of history. They include former president of Taiwan Lee Teng Hui, a graduate of Cornell University, and former mayor of Seoul Cho Soon, a graduate of the University of California at Berkeley. The economic development of Indonesia has been managed by graduates of the University of California called the "Berkeley Mafia." Many business leaders in Hong Kong, Singapore, and China have also been educated in major U.S. institutions.

Many Asians are aware of a growing fear among Americans of the increasing presence of Asians at prestigious U.S. institutions of higher education. Someone told me that these days MIT (Massachusetts Institute of Technology) stands for Made in Taiwan. A joke at Harvard University is to tell male students to "bring your own Asian" when they go out on Friday nights. However, Americans must not forget that educating international students is beneficial to their country. These students often find themselves in leadership positions when they return to their countries. Being educated at impressionable ages, many go back with favorable perceptions of Americans as future business associates. Many of them even choose to work for American subsidiaries when they return to their home countries. Because of this, Japan has recently taken a more active and strategic approach to attracting foreign students, in the hope that they will become leaders in their respective countries and have favorable views toward Japan.

Colin Powell, when he was chairman of the Joint Chiefs of Staff, said, "History and destiny have made America the...leader of the world that would be free. And the world that would be free is looking to us for inspiration.... We must play that role in whatever form...presents itself." Interestingly, while I was on a business trip to Malaysia in 2000, a local newspaper headline caught my eye. It read, "U.S. Is World's Biggest Scrooge." The opening sentence was, "As a country that is enjoying unprecedented years of prosperity, it is particularly shameful that it is one of the least generous in terms of the share of its gross domestic product devoted to helping the world's poor." The writer claimed that the Clinton administration's $10.7 billion foreign aid request for fiscal year 2001 tied a post-World War II low in the percentage of federal funds allocated to foreign aid. Quoting United Nations Secretary-General Kofi Annan, he described the U.S. government's lack of charity and consciousness of social justice as "unworthy of the traditions of this great nation."

I hope that America will continue to play a service role, sharing its financial and humanitarian wealth throughout the world.

Preservation and Conservation

In their short history, Americans have built world-class archives, museums, and parks, as if they were trying to make up for their relatively brief past. Americans want to keep whatever traditions they have. The items that Americans have collected as valuable historical mementos are beyond understanding. The Smithsonian, which celebrated its 150th anniversary in 1996, has accumulated more than 140 million American artifacts, including moon rocks, wallpaper, and the ruby red slippers Judy Garland wore in *The Wizard of Oz*. The Library of Congress in Washington, D.C., holds more information than anyone could ever fathom. The Museum of Natural History coexists with the National Museum of Folk Art. McDonald's has built a Number 1 Store Museum, and the "Newseum" is, of course, a museum of news. Libraries have been built or are being built for every president. Americans try to build the American soul into their culture.

Americans value almost any object as a memento of times past. Visiting antique stores or auctions is a favorite pastime for some. People are willing to pay top dollar for collectibles. That is why a pair of Levi's jeans from the 1940s is valued at $2,000 and a 1959 Barbie doll is worth $7,900. Many Americans spend a small fortune for antiques, and even young people have an eye for old cars and quilts. In American families, one never throws old family photographs away, and pains are taken to store them properly. An inherited grandfather clock or a mother's wedding gown is cherished. A dry cleaner in Denver told me about an elderly woman who brought in a black tuxedo. After it was dry-cleaned, the shop owner found that the fabric had melted. She reasoned that the tuxedo might have been too old to hold up to the cleaning chemicals. When the woman came to pick it up, the owner explained what had happened and offered to pay for half the replacement cost. The woman declined the offer but volunteered, "It is ninety years old. It belonged to my father, and I was going to have my grandson wear it."

Despite Americans' tendency to prefer disposable commodities, they know what to protect and how to conserve. My pastor in Korea, who was educated at Princeton University, used to say, "Americans are very protective of property. They don't use even one nail carelessly." Some Asians who rent property in the United States are perplexed when they are charged for nail holes in a wall or stains on a carpet. Americans want their properties to endure. In some countries, most properties do not last more than twenty years. People use them carelessly, do not repair them, and demolish them to put up new buildings.

Americans' attitudes toward preservation and conservation extend to cities and states. During the country's bicentennial year, the U.S. government honored five "bicentennial cities" for having preserved their culture: Washington, D.C., Boston, Philadelphia, San Antonio, and San Francisco. Americans believe that each state and every city are responsible for safeguarding the nation's heritage. Thus, many cities such as Williamsburg and Boston are preserved and honored for their traditions.

Because of numerous wars and modernization, Asians have failed to preserve important historical sites. With a history of over five thousand years, some Asians don't attach much importance to things of the past; after all, there are always many other old sites or buildings. Besides, when one must struggle with poverty, survival is more important than preserving historical artifacts for future generations.

In addition to preserving historical artifacts, Americans have made a great effort to preserve and protect their beautiful natural environment. I have traveled to many U.S. national parks, including Denali National Park in Alaska, Volcano National Park in Hawaii, Mount Rainier in Washington, the Rocky Mountains in Colorado, Shenandoah Park in Virginia, Yosemite in California, the Grand Canyon in Arizona, the El Yunque rain forest in Puerto Rico, and Virgin Islands National Park in the Caribbean. Park personnel welcomed me and other visitors with well-managed park programs and facilities. Some environmentalists may not agree with me, but I was impressed with the richness and maintenance of these resources. Rare species of trees, plants, birds, and mammals are protected across millions of acres.

Unfortunately, the industrialization of Asia has damaged natural environments and created terrible pollution in major cities. Although Asians saw nature as their friend in old times, many Asian countries have developed at the cost of their environment. As a result, pollution problems are common in many major Asian cities, and progress toward solving environmental problems has been uneven. Even in China, which started modernization and industrialization later than other Asian countries, environmental pollution and ecological destruction are serious concerns.

In the United States, there are many environmental advocacy groups that want to protect America's natural beauty. The Sierra Club is one of the oldest and largest of these groups. Formed by naturalist John Muir in 1892, the club has worked actively in political campaigns in support of proenvironment candidates and has sued corporations and cities that harm the environment. Although some Americans believe that environmentalists go overboard, it is important to recognize their contributions to improving the environment and guaranteeing biodiversity in the world. Also, they are inspiring other countries to follow suit to make the world a cleaner place for all. After all, regardless of technological accomplishments, our children will not be able to replace the planet.

Part Two

The Yin of American Culture: Liberation of American Vices

No country is perfect. With all its wealth, power, and strength, America has its weaknesses. In this part, I examine the yin of American culture, those things that cause Americans to be stressed, unhappy, alienated from society and their families, and lonely. But there is a consolation. Even though yin is the shadowy side of the slope, not all characteristics of yin are negative. Some of them were rooted in yang, but as yin energy was expanding, the positive energy was diminished and consumed. For example, obsession with time and efficiency is one negative characteristic of Americans, because it leads to exhaustion, sacrifice of family, or even loss of life. But this yin was derived from Americans' Protestant work ethic. An overemphasis on this positive (yang) energy causes a turn toward the negative because an excess of yin energy consumes the yang energy.

Another yin characteristic, insistence on rights, also started as a yang force. For founding Americans, who suffered persecution by oppressors, it was important to ensure and honor individual rights. Yet its overemphasis has caused people to forget their corresponding responsibilities. Even the overuse of lawsuits to settle disagreements started with the yang ideal of protecting individual rights. But the right to sue others has created the world's most litigious society.

So in this analysis of American vices, we should try to see them from a dualistic point of view. Many yin characteristics have the potential to be transformed into yang. All one has to do is recognize them as vices and renegotiate the balance of yin and yang energy.

Expectation of an Easy Life

Recent statistics on the number of Americans who have mental disorders is mind-boggling. One out of three Americans suffers from some sort of mental health problem, and nearly nineteen million visits are made to psychiatrists and other mental health professionals each year. Boys under the age of fifteen are significantly more likely than girls to make these visits, and women aged sixty-five or older are more frequent visitors than are men of the same age. Antidepressants are now among the most widely used drugs in America. For example, Prozac is the fifth most commonly prescribed drug. Life in the United States is no more difficult than in other countries, yet Americans rely more on mental health professionals and drugs than do others. And psychiatrists or counselors have an earlier presence in people's lives in America than they do elsewhere. For example, if a student in the U.S. dies through either an accident or suicide, his or her classmates are encouraged to see counselors. In Asia, even if a school loses scores of children through an accident, no one would consider sending the surviving children to counselors. Asians are expected to handle their grief themselves. Interestingly, it is said that American health insurance companies often prefer Asian American clients because they rely less on psychiatric visits.

For Americans, pain is bad. When an American publisher introduced a Canadian book entitled *Your Guide to Coping with Back Pain*, it had to change the title to *Conquering Back Pain* to reflect the American way of seeing pain. Pain, whether physical or emotional, is bad, so it must be conquered rather than endured. However, as Dr. M. Scott Peck stated in his best-selling book, *The Road Less Traveled*, "Life is difficult." If Americans could accept this, it would be easier for them to cope with life's challenges.

Buddhists believe that life is suffering:

> Birth is suffering, old age is suffering,
> sickness and death are suffering; to meet a
> man whom one hates is suffering; to be
> separated from a beloved one is suffering;
> to be vainly struggling to satisfy one's needs
> is suffering. In fact, a life that is not free
> from desire and passion is always involved
> with distress.[6]

Americans believe that they have to feel good all the time. For them, feeling "down" is abnormal. In an annual survey, one of every seven Americans reported suffering from some form of depression. Sadly, many of them don't know how to cope with it without resorting to medication. Once an Asian friend of mine and I read the definition of *clinically depressed*, and we laughed out loud. Both of us, who were in graduate school halfway across the world from home, fit many of the criteria. With class requirements and relationship challenges, there were times when life was difficult, even not worth living. There were some lonely nights when we would have been glad to give up living to escape from life's burdens. But that is life, and we knew that enduring it was our duty and that we must go on. The Chinese word for endurance is made up of two characters, one for a knife and the other for the heart. As students far from home, we had to bear the knives in our hearts and just get on with it.

Perhaps Asians have suffered too much in their recent history. In 1945, Japan lay in ruins from American bombs. Ten million Chinese lost their lives in the Cultural Revolution between 1966 and 1975. Koreans have suffered from the thirty-six-year Japanese occupation and the devastating Korean War, which caused a million casualties. Many Vietnamese families lost close family members during the Vietnam War. During these tragedies and hardships, Asians didn't have the luxury of asking for or expecting happiness, and they developed a mental resilience to life's bitterness. The saying "Joy is feather light, but who can carry it? Sorrow falls like a landslide, who can parry it?" illustrates Asians' tendency to accept emotional or physical pain and unhappiness as normal. Nobody told us that life would be easy or that everybody deserves happiness. Rather, Asians warn against perfect happiness, saying that if everything in one's life is perfect, even God will become jealous.

Younger Asians who have not suffered from war or poverty expect a lot more from their lives than their seniors did. They want an easy life and avoid dirty, difficult, and dangerous jobs. They want to enjoy life, not endure it. Nevertheless, they are constantly reminded of the Asian philosophical perspective on life's challenges.

As discussed earlier, in the Asian mind yin and yang coexist in everything, but there is an element of relativity: an entity regarded as yin in one light can be regarded as yang in another. A man cannot tell what is good and what is bad when things happen, because the bad can turn into the good and the good can turn into the bad. Everything is interrelated and interdependent.

With this perception, Asians are better able to cope with life's challenges. A few years ago when I was in Korea, my wallet was stolen in a subway on my way to my mother's. It was the day that my first book was released, and I wanted to deliver the first copy to my mother. The pickpocket took not only my cash but also my credit cards. Obviously disturbed, I told my mother what had happened. She reminded me of an ancient Chinese maxim, *Ho-sa-da-ma*—"for good things to happen, many bad things follow too." Later I learned that there is a similar expression in India. Interestingly, the book became a nonfiction best-seller in Korea. Of course, this kind of insight doesn't yield lost property, but it eases the distress caused by the loss. It helps people to accept life as a trade-off and to embrace good and bad as part of life. Thus, many Asians do not try to control their own destinies all the time. In a way, their fatalism also helps: unlike Americans, who blame themselves or others for what goes wrong in their lives, Asians can accept difficulties as their lot. It is easier to blame fate than themselves. As a result, they are less likely to rely on drugs, alcohol, or other artificial means of controlling their pain. They tend to believe what Chuang Tzu, the Chinese philosopher, said:

> The true men of old took life as it came,
> gladly;
> Took death as it came, without care.
>
> They had no mind to fight Tao.
> They did not try, by their own contriving
> To help Tao along.

Insistence on Rights

Once I conducted a workshop for twenty U.S. engineers on how to work with Asians. Many participants complained that their Asian counterparts sat or stood too close to them during meetings, making them feel uncomfortable. I explained how overcrowded the big cities in Asia are and how this condition affects Asians' perception of space. In Tokyo and Seoul, part-time workers are paid to push people into the subway trains during rush hours. So I asked the participants to try to see the situation from Asians' point of view and not to be offended by the "invasion of their territory." After listening to my comment, one engineer blurted out, "How can I not be offended when I am already offended?" He was not unusual. Richard Carlson, author of the Don't

Sweat the Small Stuff series, was asked to describe average Americans with two words. His answer was "easily bothered." Americans who believe in entitlement are preoccupied with their rights.

Americans' freedom has inspired many oppressed people around the world. The four essential freedoms that Franklin D. Roosevelt declared in 1941—freedom of speech and expression, freedom to worship, freedom from want, and freedom from fear—have challenged people all over the world to fight for their own rights. But now, many people in the world, and especially in Asia, say that there is too much freedom in America. "I am an American. As a taxpayer, I have the right to...," Americans often say, as if paying taxes is the only duty of citizens and entitles them to anything they want. Influenced by their country's unfettered individualism, some Americans take this insistence on their rights too far. They believe that they have license to do anything they please. "Freedom means we can do anything we like, if we don't hurt anybody else," say many.

In the name of freedom of speech and expression, some Americans say, write, and do obscene things. Others burn the U.S. flag or publish racist articles. In fact, in the name of freedom, America is losing its children to crime, drugs, sex, and alcohol. Compared with Asian youth, Americans lack discipline. In Asia, an almost militaristic discipline is inculcated. In school and at home, children in Asia are expected to follow strict rules and guidelines from an early age. There is no such thing as freedom of expression in students' choice of clothing, hair color, and body language if they don't meet school guidelines. Even coming to school with mousse in one's hair will result in disciplinary action in Korea. A few years ago, when my nephew was an eighth-grader in California, he went to Japan for a two-week exchange program. He was shocked to see how orderly the children were in the classroom. They sat straight during class, and even at recess, students walked quietly in the hall. He was also shocked to see Japanese students his age cleaning their classrooms at the end of the day. In many Asian schools, students, not workers, take turns cleaning the classrooms, hallways, windows, toilets, and other school areas. Any rights they may have as students involve corresponding duties. Although some forms of discipline are becoming less popular in Asia, this mindset is still important in every aspect of Asian life.

American citizens are indeed endowed with certain unalienable rights, among which are life, liberty, and the pursuit of happiness. Unfortunately, some stretch these rights too far; for example, a criminal actually sued a prison for emotional damage because he did not get the peanut butter he had requested. Americans need to realize that with each right comes a responsibility; they must respect others within a set of legal and moral obligations. Not all rights, if exercised, are in the interests of the people as a group. Individual rights can be maintained only when all citizens do their share in pursuit of group harmony. One has the right to be oneself within the boundaries of respect for others, but one must realize that others have that same right.

Pope John Paul II wrote that liberty was given to man not only as a gift but also as a duty and that this duty measures life. The rights and freedoms set forth in the U.S. Constitution and in federal, state, and local laws are meant to serve the people and to allow for the free and full development of each person's potential. Thus, in exercising their rights, Americans must ensure that their community's morality and order remain intact. As the late chaplain of the U.S. Senate, Peter Marshall, said, "Freedom is not the right to do as one pleases but the opportunity to please do what is right."

Part of the problem is Americans' obsession with choices. They believe that they should have choices in everything, including moral values. The danger lies in the fact that not all people are capable of making responsible choices. Some do not have the ability to avoid extremes, extravagance, and excess. People are free to go their own way, which includes being free to get hopelessly lost.

For Asians, not everything in life is a choice or preference. Instead, there are duties and responsibilities. In Japan, *on* (grace) governs one's relationship with others and with society. The Kanji character for *on* consists of three parts: the environment, the figure of a person who supports the sky, and the heart. To be a person of grace, one must know why he or she exists. *On* is an almost infinitely complicated network of responsibility, debt, and reciprocity. Individuals do not live by and for themselves. In Asian societies, people are trained to consider the needs of others (in their ingroup) before pursuing their own interests. The story of the invention of the Walkman is an excellent example. Akio Morita, former chairman of Sony, loved classical music. He wanted to find a way to listen to his music without annoying others, so he invented the Walkman. In contrast, Americans liked the Walkman because it allowed them to listen to their own favorite music without being bothered by others.

In exercising their rights, Americans must not forget their responsibilities toward others.

Refusal to Grow Up

Next to the elevator in a New York toy store, I found a sign that read, "For kids under 90." Americans seem to believe that an adult is simply a child with a grown-up body. It is not surprising, then, when adult Americans say, "The best vacation I ever had was at Disneyland." As a matter of fact, when I go to a toy store or Disneyland, I have so much fun that I don't want to leave. Adult Americans enjoy the things that are reserved for children in Asia, from cookies to roller blades. Adult Asians consider it childish to be tempted by such things.

Due to these blurred role expectations for adults and children, grown-ups have become a dying breed in America. According to writer and speaker Robert Bly, one-third of adult Americans are actually half-adults. "We have become a nation of squabbling siblings. We have abandoned our children to day-care centers and our elders to old folks homes, while we, like Peter Pan, simply 'won't grow up.'" Bly describes a culture in which Americans tolerate no one above them and show no concern for anyone below them. John Powers of the *Boston Globe* has also bemoaned the fact that there are a lot of older people, but not so many mature adults. A father of three children wears a tank top and mesh shorts on a plane trip, and women in their sixties wear sports bras as tops. In fact, I saw a father wearing a T-shirt proclaiming, "I'll never grow up." According to Powers, adults used to know what to wear and how to behave; they knew not only what to do but also what not to do. Now, however, marketers direct their pitches to these half-adults.

Americans' desire for youth is deeply embedded in their popular culture. Singers compose songs like "Forever Young," and fitness trainers encourage "Young at Heart" exercises. I admire Americans for living energetic lives, but youth is overglorified. People do not want to look their age or to be considered old. Looking old is negative. As one ad puts it, "You may grow older, but you don't have to look aged." Several prime-time television shows did features on middle-aged men who were getting plastic surgery or liposuction to look young and fit. Interviewees agreed that looking young is important for keeping their jobs in an era of corporate downsizing. Some people refuse to celebrate birthdays or to tell anyone their age because they do not want to be perceived as "over the hill." Americans seem to think that if they are not young, they are old. Because of this youth-centered culture, many Americans want to live in a stage of permanent adolescence—with the attendant lack of responsibility this implies.

The problem with overvaluing youth is that people can forget their maturity. In Asia, I have never heard of a mother eyeing her daughter's boyfriend or a father going out with his son's girlfriend. I have rarely heard of Asian teachers pursuing serious romantic and sexual relationships with their students. It is not surprising that so many American children have no adult role models in their lives and therefore look toward celebrities. Unfortunately, children see only the wealth and popularity of celebrities, not the hard work that got them where they are. Besides, many celebrities refuse to live healthy and responsible lives. Yet the lifestyles of the rich and famous rapidly become the goal for American youth.

If parents (no matter what their nationality) want their children to grow up to become mature adults, they have to be positive role models. My brother-in-law was a chain-smoker. As a doctor, he knew all the dangers of smoking, but he believed that he would rather live a shorter life enjoying what he liked than give up a harmful habit in order to live longer. Whenever his friends tried to persuade him to quit smoking, he defended it with the example of his father, who had also been a heavy smoker until he died at the age of eighty-five. One day, my nine-year-old nephew came home from school and told his father, "Dad, I don't want you to smoke. Today at school, I saw a film that showed lungs damaged by smoking. I want you to live a long time with Mom and me." His father listened with a smile, not saying a word. But from that moment on, he hasn't lit a single cigarette.

In Chinese characters, *adult* means becoming fully human. To be a full human requires certain traits. In Eastern philosophy, there are two kinds of people: big people and small people. This is not related to one's physical size. The former have more virtues than skills, and the latter have more skills than virtues. Adults are stable and reliable. They are generous and considerate; they give without thinking of getting in return. They are patient and not easily offended. They think long-term and are not controlled by the desire for instant gratification. Adults are by no means perfect, but they constantly look for ways to live better and more enlightened lives. As an Asian saying goes, "At fifty, one knows the mistakes from the past forty-nine years and vows to correct them. At sixty, one knows the mistakes of the past fifty-nine years and corrects them."

It is unfortunate that many American adults refuse to become big people. They constantly focus on self-interest, and if their desires are not fulfilled, they whine. It is fine to acknowledge and nurture the child within us, but society will regress if everybody caters to the needs of the "inner child" all the time. Asians say that if the water on the top is clean, the water at the bottom will be clean too. This means that if an older person sets a good example, the younger person will follow. Thus, American adults need to nurture their inner adults to be fully human and to set good examples for their children.

Never Slowing Down

A Fulbright scholar from Denmark told me about the discomfort she felt every Monday morning when her American colleagues would ask her what she had done over the weekend. If she said that she had just read and relaxed, they would look disappointed. Americans are action oriented; they are go-getters. They get going, get things done, and get ahead. In America, people gather for action—to play basketball, to dance, to go to a concert. When groups get together, they play games or watch videos. Many Americans don't have the patience to sit down and talk, except at a visit with a counselor or therapist. Life is in constant motion. People consider time to be wasted or lost unless they are doing something.

Clive James, an Australian journalist, observed that one of Americans' most obvious traits is the hectic pace they set for themselves. They jam a day full of activities and rush from one to another. Americans drink coffee while driving to work and checking their voice mail. Marketers are fully aware of this trend and even encourage it with "innovative" products such as the Drivetime Dribblebib—a large piece of terry cloth made for adults who drink, drive, and spill on themselves. Americans want to utilize their time efficiently in other ways also. Commuters on trains do office work on their laptop computers. They work out at the gym during lunchtime. Even while working out, they read magazines or books or watch television; many gyms now have stationary bikes with television screens, video games, and Internet connections. Americans never seem to rest their minds. On the way home from work in their cars, they listen to music or audio books or talk on cellular phones.

America never shuts down; some convenience stores, restaurants, and grocery stores never close. For busy Americans, many companies keep their toll-free numbers operating twenty-four hours a day. Americans can make their flight reservations or inquire about their long-distance phone bills in the middle of the night. (In other countries, stores close much earlier, and customer service departments operate only during the daytime.)

Now, thanks to technology, many Americans are expected to check their messages, respond to pagers, or send e-mail after regular work hours, during the weekend, and even while they are on vacation. Americans go to seminars on time management or read books on this subject to learn how to use their time even more efficiently. In contrast, given their preoccupation with time, I am always amazed to see them patiently waiting in line to get into a popular movie or to be seated at a busy restaurant.

Thanks to American influence, Asians have started to realize that time is a resource to be carefully managed, but most don't believe that their lives should be organized minute by minute. In many Asian countries, it is hard to find a desk calendar with a section for every fifteen-minute segment of the day, similar to the ones used in America. The popularity of the one-minute series in America—one-minute manager, one-minute father, one-minute mother, one-minute lover, and even one-minute wisdom—is a reflection of a culture that values time. Given their tight schedules and numerous activities, one minute is often all that can be spared. With so much emphasis on efficiency and productivity, life is always busy: go, go, go. It is no coincidence that Americans invented fast food; time is far too important to waste on eating. *Reader's Digest* and *People* magazine are also reflections of Americans' obsession with saving time: they provide condensed novels and stories.

People in Eastern cultures believe that if there is no time, they can make time. Thus, Americans find it relatively easy to make an appointment with an Asian executive on short notice. Unlike his American counterpart's, his calendar is flexible, allowing him to meet people as needed. Every minute of his life is not scheduled far in advance. When Asians meet for lunch or dinner, the event is not over as soon as the meal is finished; they give themselves enough time to catch up with each other's lives. It is common to spend a whole evening visiting with a friend or client. Even more important, it is okay to do nothing. Punctuality and productivity are flexible. As the saying goes, the Chinese are extremely punctual, provided you give them plenty of time. They always finish a thing on schedule, provided the schedule is long enough.

Despite all their convenience items and timesaving devices, most Americans will never have enough time. Unless they change their perspectives on time and life, their lives will continue to be hectic and stressful, and they will rush themselves to the grave. Americans' constant activity may be the reason why the country has become a superpower in such a short time, but "life's prize is not always to the swift in the race."

To appreciate life and find peace, Americans must learn to quiet their minds. According to Zen Buddhism, people can reach enlightenment through extended periods of meditation. By meditating in silence, people have the opportunity to clear their minds so that their real nature can shine through. A Buddhist monk once told me that the mind is like a pond and that the pond reflects the world. When the mind is calm and peaceful, the pond is still and we can see an accurate reflection of the world. But if the mind is agitated, busy with distraction and stimulation, the water ripples, giving us distorted images of the world. When this happens, our reactions to the world become distorted and our relationships with others are out of balance. Indeed, the Chinese character for being busy has two components: one means to destroy and the other means the heart. Making your life overly hectic destroys your heart and causes you to lose yourself.

Americans who live at a fast, unwavering pace without any peace of mind would do well to listen to the Taoist writer Chuang Tzu: "To go nowhere and do nothing is the first step toward finding peace in the Tao [the Way]."

Obsession with Control

Americans are obsessed with controlling their destiny, from health to happiness. They want to prepare themselves for life's events. In case their marriage doesn't work out, couples sign prenuptial agreements, which are nonexistent in most other countries. In case they might be sued for any reason, professionals purchase malpractice insurance. As soon as the manufacturer's three-year or 36,000-mile warranty for my car had expired, I received a brochure for insurance that would cover me up to 60,000 or 100,000 miles. Americans are persuaded to be prepared for virtually anything through various types of insurance. My parents never had insurance for any home they have owned in the past fifty years. They still don't have it, and they are not an exception. Until the government provided health care for the elderly, my parents had no medical insurance either. They just lived one day at a time.

Besides trying to control their fate, Americans are obsessed with controlling their health. A dental hygienist recommended that I get my teeth cleaned every four months. Even though I have very good teeth, she also recommended an ultrasonic toothbrush that would help keep my teeth and gums even healthier. I already use a special toothbrush for wisdom teeth, floss, and mouthwash, which I didn't know existed before I came to the United States. I can't help thinking that half the world's population has never seen a dentist, and many people have never tasted toothpaste.

Some Americans doubt the safety of the air they breathe or the water they drink inside their houses. They set up special equipment to filter the air and purify the water. They install carpets made of natural fabric rather than artificial weave. They use mite-proof mattresses and pillow covers to keep dust-mite allergens away from their skin and out of their respiratory tracts. Asians say that if people are too particular and picky about cleanliness, they will die earlier than normal because of their obsession. Interestingly, researchers are now finding that Americans' excessive cleanliness causes them to get sick more often because they lose the good bacteria in their bodies and weaken their ability to fight germs. People who have such difficult-to-please personalities will never have peace of mind and will die young from stress. Many Americans spend a fortune to maintain youthful bodies, trying to deny aging and death. But they forget about enjoying life, and their exercise, hygiene, and special diets become burdens rather than benefits.

Another American obsession is safety control. When I was pregnant, I was overwhelmed with information and advice on a month-by-month basis: take prenatal vitamins daily, attend breathing classes, complete several checklists from month to month. After I delivered my baby, I was bombarded with information about parenting dos and don'ts and many gadgets for baby care and safety, including a baby-wipes warmer, an oven lock, and a toilet-seat latch. I was also invited to baby-safety workshops. Although the items on sale there seemed to be safer than the off-the-shelf products, I could not see paying a two-hundred-dollar premium for a crib or a high chair to reduce the remote chance of my child falling from one of them. From my Asian perspective, it was a bit too much. Of course, cost is never too high when a life is at stake, but if I had bought everything suggested to me and taken every precaution, I would have been sick from stress. We need to use common sense and then accept the rest as fate. Even if parents take all the precautions they can for their children, if things are going to happen, they will happen. There are freak accidents that are impossible to prevent. Thus, Asians say that if a baby is going to die, he might die by drowning in a small rice bowl filled with water.

Americans want to control everything around them, and this tendency often makes them difficult to work with in international business. In drawing up a contract, Americans include contingency plans for everything that could possibly happen. Recently, one of my clients asked me to sign an indemnity agreement that the firm's lawyers had prepared. I had already signed a contract and a nondisclosure agreement that described the scope and conditions of my work in detail. At another Fortune 500 company, I had to propose a needs assessment for my workshop participants and have the questionnaire reviewed by corporate legal counsel before its distribution.

When I worked in Asia, my clients and I understood that we worked in good faith and that mutual understanding was enough. Most Asians know that things change. If something unexpected happens, the matter is usually resolved in a way that pleases both parties. Of course, conflicts are not always resolved in a peaceful manner, but most Asians do not try to predict or prevent all possibilities in advance. They take things as they come and use their common sense. Americans must be willing to surrender a measure of their rationality and control so that they can reap the gifts of the soul and learn to accept life.

In 1937, Chinese philosopher Lin Yutang shared his insights on how to relax and overcome obsession.

> American engineers in building bridges calculate so finely and exactly as to make the two ends come together within one-tenth of an inch. But when the two Chinese begin to dig a tunnel from both sides of a mountain, both come out on the other side. The Chinese's firm conviction is that it doesn't matter so long as a tunnel is dug through, and if we have two instead of one, why, we have a double track to boot. Provided you are not in a hurry, two tunnels are as good as one, dug somehow, finished somehow and if the train can get through somehow.[7]

Too Many Choices

If Patrick Henry were alive today, he would come up with a new motto, "America, give me a choice or give me death." In the book *The Stuff Americans Are Made Of*, authors Josh Hammond and James Morrison identify the seven cultural forces that define Americans today. First on their list is insistence on choice. When we think about the founders of this country and the immigrants who chose to adopt America as their home, it is only natural for Americans to be preoccupied with choice.

For almost anything—homes, cars, appliances, tooth-brushes, books, movies, cable channels, stamps, and food—Americans have more choices than any other people in the world. In buying a home, Americans can choose different styles, floor plans, and landscapes. If they can't find an existing home they like, they will custom-design a new one. In many Asian countries, building a dream home is un-heard-of for most home owners. Unless they are very rich, most families are happy just to have a place to call home. When Americans buy cars, they have endless options: make, model, size, color, features, tinted glass, price range, and on and on. Again, if no car on the lot meets their requirements, they can order a custom-designed car.

Having choices is not always fun, however. The sheer number of choices can be overwhelming. When buying something as simple as a toothbrush, American consumers have options—color, size, shape, design, and bristle stiff-ness (hard, medium, soft). Grocery stores have soda, ice cream, chips, and juice in seemingly endless flavors. For-eign visitors are shocked not only at the abundance of American stores but also at the variety of products available. Despite these ample choices, food companies continue to give Americans even more choice with new and improved products along with the original ones.

Being so accustomed to having options, Americans de-mand choices even when they are not offered. One French chef observed that Americans often demand substitute ingredients for their entrees, regardless of the chef's exper-tise, whereas Europeans leave the cooking to the chef. According to Phil Patton, author of *Made in America*, "The great American products have always sought to enable the individual to distinguish and improve himself. Even when mass-produced and universally owned, American products were aimed at magnifying the power of the individual."

Yet not everybody appreciates such empowerment. An Asian man who came to America on a business trip shared his agony over having to make choices everywhere he turned. On the first day he arrived, he went to a deli to get a sandwich. First, he was shocked to see so many varieties of sandwiches on the menu. Then, when he ordered a ham and cheese sandwich, the clerk asked what kind of bread he wanted, what kind of ham, what kind of cheese, what vegetables, what dressing, and so on. He could barely communicate in English and had no idea what the clerk was asking. He said that the experience was so agonizing and time-consuming that he avoided going to delis for six months.

To meet the expectations of choice-driven consumers, American manufacturers and service providers go way beyond the necessities, although the choices often come with additional costs to consumers. At the grocery check-out, customers are asked to choose between plastic and paper bags. If they want to get their car washed, they are likely to be asked to select their options—with or without wax, towel- or air-dried, underbody wash or regular wash. My fitness center offers more than fifteen different kinds of classes—yoga, taekwondo, high-impact aerobics, low-impact aerobics, waterobics, boxerobics, salsarobics (with a Latin American beat), step'n sculpt, cardiofunk (dancing to a loud and fast beat), and many more.

To a certain extent, having choices is a boon. I must admit that when I travel abroad, I often miss being able to choose diet soda or flavored sparkling water, for example.

Nevertheless, too many choices give consumers as many headaches as comforts. They stagger under sensory overload and waste their time and energy making decisions about what columnist Dave Barry calls "annoying inventions." One British woman said that she would be glad to return to her country because she would be able to shop at the supermarket without agonizing over which of twenty flavors of yogurt she should buy. Americans may feel empowered by having choices, but true empowerment comes from the sense of knowing what we are doing. Having no choice can be a blessing at times.

A few enlightened corporations have shifted to simplicity. Diaper companies, for example, produce one-color (unisex) diapers, instead of using pink for girls and blue for boys. It is time that Americans relinquish their preoccupation with choices and come to realize that letting go of choices is a liberating experience. By simplifying their options, they can save money and reduce headaches. I used to agonize over choices when making purchases. Now I remember the advice my friend gave me within two weeks of my arrival in the United States: "In America, all you have to decide is how much you want to spend." I used to pay a premium to buy top-of-the-line products with lots of features, but I found myself using only the basic features. For example, my washing machine has seven cycles, three temperature settings, and several other fancy features, but I use only one setting. Maybe my laundry is not cleaned right, but so far, no one has noticed. For people like me, there is no point in paying extra. Besides, more features also mean more complications and repairs, for complexity breeds problems.

Wastefulness

Once I read that if the whole world wanted to adopt the American lifestyle, five planet Earths would be needed. The United States, with less than 5 percent of the world's population, consumes 34 percent of the world's energy and a similar share of other commodities.

Those who have traveled outside the United States realize how much Americans take abundance and comfort for granted. So many things are freely given, and these free items encourage waste. At restaurants, Americans expect free napkins, utensils, ketchup, mustard, or other condiments. Restaurants in Japan or Hong Kong give customers very tiny napkins, and even those are not always provided automatically. In many parts of Europe, patrons have to pay extra for ketchup, soy sauce, or other condiments. In Belgium, I bought an order of chicken nuggets for my son and had to pay for the first packet of ketchup. Recognizing my American accent and feeling sorry for my culture shock, the cashier said, "Unlike in America, the only things free in Belgium are sunshine and smiles."

Americans expect to find free public rest rooms fully equipped with toilet paper, soap, and, ideally, disposable toilet-seat covers. In Europe, people must often pay to use public rest rooms, even in some restaurants. If they want a toilet-seat cover, they have to buy one in a vending machine. People cannot expect soap, toilet paper, or paper towels in all public rest rooms in Asia, either.

Americans take comfortable temperatures for granted in buildings and public transportation. Most buildings in America provide air-conditioning in the summer and central heating in the winter. In other countries, this is not always so. Even in affluent Asian countries such as Japan and Singapore, not all public places are air-conditioned. Even if they are, they are maintained at energy-saving temperatures. Once I visited an aquarium in Sydney, Australia. Although it was summer there, this world-class aquarium hadn't turned on the air-conditioning.

Blessed with abundance, Americans waste a lot, from energy to paper. Some buildings are lit twenty-four hours a day, even when nobody is using them. Some air-conditioned buildings maintain such low temperatures that people have to wear sweaters in the summer. American cars are much bigger than Asian or European cars, and most Americans commute alone in them. Free and abundant informational brochures are also a source of waste. From the IRS to banks, from libraries to car dealers, many forms and brochures are distributed free of charge. If they were sold, would people take as many forms as they take now? Reportedly, 3.8 million tons of junk mail are delivered annually in America. Products delivered by mail are carefully wrapped and packaged to minimize damage, creating waste. For example, a CD-ROM might come in a box that is three or four times larger than the disk.

Americans enjoy the lowest prices for consumer items from all over the world. Wal-Mart customers can get 109 photos for $3.95—but who really needs 109 photos? Maybe it reduces unit cost, but what a waste. Compared with other countries, in America, most things are available so cheaply that people don't have to think twice about purchasing them—and discarding them. When I go to a discount warehouse, I look at the amount of things some people carry in their carts. Maybe they shop only once a month, but their carts look like they are preparing for a war. People tend to use a product more frivolously when there is more of it. When I go to Korea, I watch carefully what I throw away. There are no twenty- or thirty-gallon trash bags. The trash bags sold in the market (government-enforced) are a little bigger than U.S. plastic grocery bags, and they don't hold much.

I admire many Americans for their efforts to reduce waste and recycle faithfully. To discourage waste, many cities are adopting pay-as-you-throw policies. Some schools prohibit children from using disposable bags or utensils. A couple of buffet restaurants in Los Angeles have adopted a policy of fining those who waste food; customers pay a premium if they leave unfinished food on their plates. Although these efforts are admirable, they are not enough to make Americans waste less. According to the *World Press Review*, the average American consumes (and throws out) so much that the environmental impact is equivalent to that of a country of four billion people.

The containers used for take-out food are huge for the amount of food they hold, and most of them are not recyclable. Parties and holidays also create an incredible amount of trash because people decorate for the occasions with unrecyclable materials, exchange gifts with double or triple wrapping, and use disposable tableware.

Despite most Americans' environmental consciousness, they are not willing to give up their conveniences for the sake of their environment. When environmental activists called out the troops for a protest against sport utility vehicles (SUVs) in Detroit one summer, only fifteen protesters came.

If Americans realize that all the things at their disposal come with a price, they will be much more careful about what they waste. Even a loaf of bread reaches the consumer through many hardworking people: a farmer who sweats under the sun, a trucker who transports the flour with little sleep, a baker who rises early every morning to make the bread, and a checkout clerk who works at minimum wage. When they want to throw away one piece of bread, they should remember the toil and time that was invested in it. And even in the United States, there are children who go to bed hungry at night.

Too Much Ownership, Too Little Enjoyment

It is not surprising that Americans complain that they have no time for anything. They spend much of their time shopping and working to pay for all the things they purchase. A newlywed couple who had bought a three-bedroom house complained that they were running out of space—and they didn't have any children. With their dual income and credit cards, they bought so many things for the house that their acquisitions outgrew their two-thousand-square-foot space. Their two-car garage and storage space were not large enough to hold all their things. I predict that as soon as they move to a bigger home, they will need even more space. Many people don't put their cars in the garage because it's being used for storage.

Compared with Asians, most Americans enjoy the comfort of large homes, but many of them dream about even bigger homes. Then, as soon as they have their dream house, they want a vacation home. Owning both a dream house and a vacation home means that families have to spend more time working to pay for them. They have to fill the vacation home with more purchases and maintain both properties. One gentleman who owns a weekend home on a lake told me that he had bought the property twenty years ago, thinking that he would enjoy weekends there. But after countless weeks of working to decorate the place, he finally realized that he wasn't enjoying the property much.

Americans own a lot of things. Whenever I visit American homes, I am amazed at what families own—multiple cars, television sets, CD players, and so on. More than 90 percent of U.S. households have cars; 40 percent of those have two or more. Even households with annual incomes of less than twenty thousand dollars are likely to have a VCR, an answering machine, and cable television. Bathrooms are overflowing with matching accessories and body products. Closets are replete with unworn clothes and shoes. Children's rooms are filled with toys, videos, and sports memorabilia. Storage areas are packed with seasonal items. Walls are crowded with pictures and decorations. Shopping has become America's most popular pastime, along with sports, and it has become an addiction or therapy for some. Outlet malls and car dealers display the Stars and Stripes and encourage Americans to shop as if shopping were an act of patriotism. As a result, Americans are not ashamed of their shopping indulgence or materialistic orientation. I once saw a bumper sticker that read, "If you don't know that money can buy happiness, you don't know where to shop."

Americans love collecting stuff. From early childhood, they learn to collect. From kids'-meal toys to baseball cards to Beanie Babies, American children acquire the habit of collecting things. Every week, fast-food chains provide specials with collectibles carrying the message, "Collect all four." As soon as that is over, there is another promotion. It's mind-boggling to see how much stuff American kids have in their rooms. They continue to collect throughout their lifetime. When they become adults, they quickly surrender to the temptation to collect anything from gadgets to plates, from electric trains to miniature dollhouses.

Marketers fully exploit Americans' proclivity for buying more than they need. Hollywood provides both adults and children with movie-theme products, from clothing to backpacks to mugs to school supplies. Publishers encourage readers to collect best-selling series such as the immensely popular Harry Potter series and the Chicken Soup for the Soul series. Although there were already many "flavors," more kept coming, including "soups" for pet lovers. Many other best-sellers and movies are followed by merchandise, including calendars, cups, T-shirts, and even trivia games.

Americans' average annual personal income is nearly sixty-five times the average income of half of the world's population. Despite poverty in inner cities, Americans enjoy a more comfortable lifestyle than people anywhere else. Even when Americans envied Japan for its economic power in the 1980s, they enjoyed a higher standard of living than the Japanese. Yet Americans want even more.

I believe in pursuing wealth, but I also believe that life must be balanced. Maybe I'm still under the influence of traditional Asian antimaterialistic ideals. Although the Chinese always valued wealth, money has been downplayed in Asia. In Asian novels, the rich were often portrayed as evil men. People were warned against acquiring sudden wealth;

they were told that it would bring disaster. Although Asians are becoming more materialistic, the concept of honest poverty has long been admired.

Even though some Americans believe that material things can bring them happiness, possessions are not always a blessing. According to a survey, 51 percent of parents say that their children (aged two to seventeen) have televisions in their bedrooms. Some parents allow children to have their own VCRs. Other families spend most evenings playing computer games or surfing the Internet on their multiple computers. This means less time spent together as a family. If there is only one television in the house, family members can at least be in the same room and talk about what they are watching. In a large home, parents and children often don't know what other family members are doing. Every family member has his or her own separate life.

To simplify their lifestyle, Americans need not look to the East. American philosopher Henry David Thoreau said, "Most of the luxuries and many of the so-called comforts of life are not only dispensable, but positive hindrances to the elevation of mankind." Before Americans become slaves to their possessions, they might want to ask what they can live without and how they can enjoy life and their families more.

Obsession with Big

Everything is so big in America. The country is big, companies are big, stores are big, houses are big, even the people are big. In my home state, Texas, we often say that you can drive all day long and still be in Texas. It took me almost seven hours to fly from Dallas to Anchorage, while it took the Japanese coming from Tokyo six hours to reach Anchorage. So we have to accept that Americans are used to a lot of space and everything on a big scale.

Yet Americans' infatuation with bigness doesn't necessarily stem from being in a big country. According to Josh Hammond and James Morrison, authors of *The Stuff Americans Are Made Of*, to Americans, the big and the best achieve mythical proportions that transcend the dictionary definitions. Every month or so, we hear news of the biggest merger in history. American companies are already enormous, but they want to get even bigger. Soon, there may be only one or two companies in each industry. There are already many megastores and superstores that stock big items in large quantities. American marketers often fail to sell their products—from detergent to juice—overseas because they are too big. In many countries, women shop on a daily basis and carry purchases by hand. Big American stores claim, "We buy big so that you can save big." But they are overwhelming to many people. Maybe I don't go to megastores often enough to familiarize myself with the layout, but I get lost or distracted wandering down cavernous aisles with items stacked to the ceilings.

Americans want big homes, too. According to one study, the American dream has gone upscale: one acre of land and six thousand square feet of living space. In 1997, the median American house was 1,975 square feet, compared with 700 square feet in Japan. Of course, space is a prized commodity in big U.S. cities like New York and Chicago, but it is no secret that Americans want as much space as they can afford.

Recently I was in northern California, just outside Sacramento. Since my childhood dream was to be an architect,

I'm interested in buildings and houses. The locals recommended three areas for home sight-seeing that were relatively newly developed. I was amazed to see how many homes looked liked Beverly Hills mansions, or even better. There were not just a couple of them, but hundreds, and this was not something uniquely Californian, either. There are similar neighborhoods in every state and many cities in the United States. In other countries, only the very rich, often business tycoons or influential politicians, can own such beautiful properties. What is unique about modern America is that the people who dream about and own such places are ordinary people who describe themselves as upper middle class.

Next to or adjoining their big houses, Americans build three- to four-car garages to house their cars, which are also getting bigger. American cars are already much larger than Japanese or European cars. The popularity of SUVs and trucks is mind-boggling. In 1999, the market share of new SUVs was almost 50 percent. In Asia, only people with moving or delivery businesses own such vehicles.

In Asia, most things are small. Many countries are small in size. Japan, with a population equal to almost half that of the United States, is the size of California. South Korea is one-seventh the size of Texas but has more than double its population. Hong Kong also has one of the highest population densities per square mile. Given limited land, houses are small. Japanese often complain that they make the fanciest high-tech appliances in the world, but they don't have the space to put them in their home. Of course, affluent people and those who live in the suburbs can enjoy more space, but they don't have an obsession with big as being better. Since space is an expensive commodity, stores can't afford to carry large items. Drinks are also much smaller—coffee cups, soda cans, and juice containers, to name a few. Snacks don't come in a huge family size. And people don't get too big either.

Americans are getting bigger, though. American adults are 25 percent heavier than they were in 1990. Children are an inch taller and 30 percent heavier than they were twenty years ago. It is also estimated that in a few years, half of the American women over age eighteen will wear a size fourteen or larger. The market for full-figured women is the fastest-growing segment in women's clothing. When I came to America, what I enjoyed most was that I didn't have to be self-conscious about my weight any more.

To accommodate big Americans in their big houses, manufacturers produce large furniture, appliances, and accessories. American bathrooms are big. Bath towels are big. Appliances are big. One American woman in Germany wrote to her friends, "Everything else here is miniature—refrigerators, washers, dryers, etc. It takes five loads of wash here, and back home maybe two." Furnishings are big. According to a *Wall Street Journal* article entitled "You're Not Smaller; Your Chair Is Bigger," home furniture gets larger to match expanding egos and waistlines. The size of an American sofa is almost the size of a bedroom in another country.

What's wrong with this penchant for bigness? Waste. Huge homes and cars require more energy. Servings of food are so big that much is thrown away. Sometimes I go to restaurants patronized by elderly people and am amazed at how much they are given to eat. A lot of them don't have an active lifestyle, but they are given the same amount of food as active adults. There are kids' meals for half price, so why not offer an elderly portion for half price? Instead of giving a senior citizen's discount for a regular meal, restaurants could offer a smaller meal for a reduced price.

Unhealthy and Overindulgent Eating

"Welcome to America! If you don't watch what you eat, you'll gain ten pounds during the first semester because food is so fattening and sweet." This was the first warning I got from my Korean friends when I arrived in the United States for my graduate education. Recently I had an opportunity to train Asian engineers on living and working in America. When I asked them what they would like to adopt from America, there were a variety of answers, from freedom to space. When I asked them what they would not want to take home from America, the answer was unanimous—junk food. Although they enjoy one of the highest living standards in the world, Americans' eating habits are unhealthy and even destructive. Most Americans consume food with too much fat, too much salt, too much sugar, too many chemicals, and many empty calories.

From childhood to adulthood, many Americans eat unhealthy diets. Since they know that the foods they eat are not nutritious, they take supplements or vitamins. Americans have all the resources (except the time to cook or enjoy good meals) to treat themselves to tasty, nutritious meals, but most people don't utilize the abundant supply of quality food and the biggest and best-stocked kitchens in the world. Instead of healthy homemade meals, they eat frozen entrees. Instead of drinking water or tea with their meals, many drink soda with sugar or sweetener, neither of which is healthful. Instead of fresh vegetables, many buy only frozen or canned vegetables, because of the convenience. As a working mother, I have tried them and understand how easy it is to rely on them. But once I found that canned spinach had almost no vitamin C and that frozen vegetables contained very little nutrition, I dropped prepared vegetables from my diet.

Americans also consume large amounts of artificial products, including artificial flavors, colors, and preservatives. Although increasing numbers of Americans are into health foods and organic produce, the majority continue to eat diets that are not conducive to good health.

When Americans eat out, they are given unhealthy choices. Restaurants serve soups that are too salty or fatty, accompanied by salted crackers or bread and butter. Many entrees are fried and come with french fries or baked potato with sour cream.

Even new mothers don't get special food after delivering babies. In Asia, they are given special diets to replenish the loss of blood and water. According to the yin-yang principle, every food has yin and yang properties and should be eaten in balanced proportions. Chinese doctors have been using the principle to cure diseases for more than two thousand years, because all foods have special medicinal effects. Yin foods are bland and low in calories and have a cooling effect on the body. In contrast, yang foods are rich and spicy and warm the body. Boiling makes food yin, and deep-frying makes it yang. Based on this philosophy, most American diets are extreme yang and therefore unbalanced. A renowned Chinese chef once lamented that dishes at U.S.

Chinese restaurants had been adapted to meet the demands of the lowest denominator.

Quality is not the only problem with Americans' diet. Quantity is definitely a big factor. The amount of food that Americans consume at a single sitting can be astounding to both Asians and Europeans: one-pound steaks, a sixteen-inch double-pan pizza, extra-large french fries, Super Big Gulps, twenty-ounce bags of chips, and foot-long submarine sandwiches are some of the gastronomic heavyweights found from corner stores to supermarkets in America. In other countries, food is not packaged or served in such huge sizes. For especially self-indulgent diners, America offers all-you-can-eat restaurants for breakfast, lunch, and dinner. Despite the many low-fat, nonfat, and sugar-free products, Americans don't lose weight because of the quantities they eat. Based on my personal observations, I have concluded that people tend to eat double when they know their food is low in fat or fat free.

When it comes to food, the blessing of abundance can be a curse; it encourages health problems. In a study of mice, one researcher found that overeating accelerates the aging process. It's no wonder that antiaging products are popular in America. One out of every three adults and one out of every four children in America are overweight. According to *U.S. News & World Report*, in 1999 there were 58 million overweight or obese people in the United States. One may ask what is so bad about obesity—it harms only the person him- or herself. However, the health risks involved in being overweight increase the cost of health care.

When I came to this country, I was baffled as to why some Americans who lived in poverty were fat. I was surprised to learn that being overweight was more of a problem for the underclass than for the upper class. In Asia, I had always associated poor people with thinness. When I saw impoverished people in Third World countries, most of them were very thin due to malnutrition. Some argue that underprivileged Americans can't afford to buy lean meat or low-fat products and instead buy filling and inexpensive foods that are high in carbohydrates.

What is even more amazing about Americans is that they eat everywhere—in their cars, at the movies, in classes, on the streets. In other countries, there are appropriate times and places to eat. And Americans do not share their food. Asian visitors are often shocked when their American peers eat their snacks without offering to share them. Asians always offer to share with the people around them. Even if they have only one piece of gum, they divide it in half. The late actress Audrey Hepburn said, "If you want a slim figure, share your food with the hungry." French acquaintances have told me that the reason they stay so fit despite their wonderful cuisine is that they don't eat snacks between meals. I'm not suggesting that Americans give up all their snacks, but if they shared their midafternoon snacks and munchies, they would also enjoy friendship, maintain their weight, and safeguard their health.

Lack of Loyalty

Recently a long-distance telephone company representative called me and said, "If you switch to our company today, we'll give you eleven thousand airline miles." I told him I had to decline the offer because I had accepted a one-hundred-dollar promotion certificate from my current provider only a month ago. I added that I wanted to give my current provider time to recover its money. He replied, "It's very noble of you to think that way, but some people change their provider on a daily basis." According to Frederick F. Reichheld, author of *The Loyalty Effect* and director of Bain & Company, a management consulting firm, U.S. corporations lose half their customers in five years, half their employees in four years, and half their suppliers in less than one year. He warns that at its current rate, this lack of product and services loyalty stunts corporate performance by 25 to 50 percent.

Most Asians find it difficult to understand how American CEOs can increase their own salaries exorbitantly while laying people off. In Asia, a layoff is not a simple business decision; there is often a moral obligation to keep loyal employees as long as possible. Relations between employers and employees are often like those within a family. The junior and senior staff consult with and help one another in good times and bad. This doesn't mean that Asian companies never let employees go. Some Japanese and Korean corporations have already introduced early-retirement options to employees who had expected lifelong employment. Yet it is rare to lay off thousands of people at once to please Wall Street or stockholders. As U.S. companies become less loyal to their employees, workers become less loyal to their companies. They constantly shop around, looking for a better deal, a higher salary, and more attractive benefits. Employers' lack of loyalty to their employees also damages morale. A company supervisor shared with me how a layoff had affected her department. Her staff felt that they had to compete with one another to keep their jobs. Everybody was considered an enemy, and staff members were no longer able to trust one another.

Similarly, how can American CEOs expect loyalty from their employees when they are paid 128 times more than most of their workers? In Japan, the ratio of an average employee's salary to the CEO's salary is 1:16, and in Germany, it is 1:26. Although some companies such as Microsoft, Dell, and other high-tech corporations have done a great job in rewarding their employees through profit sharing, they are exceptions rather than norms.

The loyalty problem does not stop at American corporations; American families also suffer from a lack of loyalty. Over and over again I hear about women who are devastated when their husbands tell them that they are in love with someone else. Asian men and women walk away, too, but not as frequently as Americans do. My Asian friends often say laughingly, "How dare my husband desert a wife who bore him two sons?" Men jokingly respond, "Who would want my wife when she has a husband and two children?" Sadly, adultery exists in Asia, and some people never recover their sense of trust once they find out about a spouse's affair. Yet Asian marriages usually survive, because most husbands and wives believe that it is their destiny to be together. They may give their bodies to someone else, but not their souls.

Having known many good people who are divorced, I accept the fact that people often separate from their spouses, for a variety of reasons. However, what I don't understand is the backbiting that occurs after the separation. It is sad enough to end a marriage, but why do people feel compelled to prove that they are better than their "exes"? Ex-wives or

-lovers of celebrities often bad-mouth their former mates publicly—from Loni Anderson to Dennis Rodman. Americans reveal details about their "exes," and if they can get some money by telling their story, they are willing to do so—in intimate detail.

When Gennifer Flowers' story came out during the 1992 presidential campaign, an Asian businessman commented, "She must have been treated very badly to go public like that." Asian men often have mistresses, but afterward, the "other women" rarely publicly criticize the men to whom they were attached. A few American friends have explained that it is un-American to turn down an opportunity to make a buck. If they can earn quick money by selling their stories, why not? "In America everything and everyone is a commodity to be bought and to be sold for dollars," observed a British writer. In Asia, women who have affairs may keep quiet because of a threat or due to shame, but they also feel a sense of loyalty to the person they were involved with. In Confucian cultures, loyalty is a key value. One should be loyal to one's spouse, employer, parents, and friends.

Certainly there are loyal Americans who have stayed with their employers, spouses, and friends through good times and bad. They endure inconveniences and resist the temptation to make a profit. Americans can be exceptionally loyal, especially to their sports teams. The New York Yankees and San Francisco 49ers, for example, have many lifelong, die-hard fans. Communities and colleges have also been able to rely on the support of their loyal citizens and alumni in times of need. So maybe Americans' challenge is a matter of expanding their loyalty to a wider network.

Impersonal Relationships

Many outsiders find American relationships to be too superficial. One of the complaints Europeans and Asians have
about Americans is that it's difficult to become real friends
with them. Americans are very friendly on the surface, but
they don't reveal their inner selves. One Japanese American compared Americans with the Japanese: Americans are
friendly and easy to get to know; however, they have only
surface-level friendships. They are peach soft on the outside
but have a hard pit inside. They are always protecting
something of a personal or professional nature, and they do
not tend to make themselves vulnerable. In contrast, the
Japanese are like coconuts; it is very hard to crack their
shells and get to know them. That shell is formality, which
they use to decide with whom they wish to develop a
relationship. Once the shell is broken, however, their affection spills all over, and they would gladly give their friends
all they have. The Japanese are willing to make themselves
vulnerable.

Americans are task oriented. People at work don't spend
much time getting to know one another. Rarely do people go
out together after work unless there is a visiting client or a
company function. When their interaction is limited to
business only, people do not have fun working together.
Some people even say, "If it weren't for people, work would
be fun." Workers in smaller organizations tend to have
closer relationships than those in larger ones, but the level
of closeness is still low in the opinion of Asians. Partly due
to their hectic schedules, many Americans claim they
cannot afford to spend time with business associates. In

Asia, people are more involved with one another on a personal level. When they meet people for business, efficiency is not the only goal; they want to have some personal connection. Workers frequently go out together and get to know personal details about their co-workers, such as what their parents do, where they live, what schools they attended, and so forth. Chinese sociologist Fei Xiaotong observed that Americans regard all relationships as contracts. In a contractual society, relationships can be terminated whenever one party chooses. Thus, some Americans perceive any relationship, including marriage, as impermanent and don't want to invest much energy or emotion in it.

These differences foster misunderstanding in both Americans and Asians when they start working together. Americans prefer transaction to interaction. When they go to an Asian country, they often feel frustrated with the slow progress of the business side of things. Although they appreciate Asians' hospitality—such as treating them to fabulous dinners and showing them around the country—Americans are anxious to initiate meetings to discuss business. They want to share all the data they have brought and close the deal, not take the time to get to know their business partners. In fact, when I asked executives in Hong Kong about the most common mistake made by their American counterparts, they answered, "Americans want to talk about business too soon, within the first five minutes of a meeting."

This business-first approach leads Asians to believe that Americans are not interested in building personal relationships, and when Asians come to the United States, they feel that they are treated poorly by their busy American counterparts. Rarely are they picked up at the airport, and they are left alone most evenings and weekends. Having experienced such treatment, an Asian businessman told me that for him, negotiation starts at the airport. If his business partner picks him up at the airport, he immediately has good feelings toward the American. If he is left to fend for himself with a rental car and a map, the negotiation will not proceed as smoothly.

Recently I was invited to an American company as a consultant. The meeting started at noon at the client's site. There were no drinks, no sandwiches—nothing. If I had been in Asia, they would have asked me whether I had eaten lunch or suggested that we have lunch before getting down to business. I would not have charged for the advice I gave during lunch, and the clients could have gotten a better deal. For Asians, sharing a meal is like sharing a common bond. Eating together is traditionally one of their most cherished rituals. In contrast, many Americans eat lunch alone in their cubicles or use lunchtime for running errands.

This efficiency orientation has contributed to the rapid growth of impersonal communication devices. Even talking to someone on the phone at an American workplace is a rare treat these days because of voice mail and electronic menus. It is a fact that some workers hardly ever answer their phones. They either have caller ID to screen their calls or keep their voice mail on all the time, then return calls at their convenience. They think that this is efficient time management, but such a practice is considered very impersonal by internationals. In most countries, even developed ones, calls are answered by live human beings. Co-workers pick up others' calls to take messages. In contrast, some

Americans avoid personal contact as much as possible, even sending e-mail to peers sitting next to them. One cartoon reads, "If e-mail, fax, pager, or voice mail doesn't work, you can come down and talk to me." Many Asians don't see the American way as being more efficient. In Asia, if employees have questions, they often walk down the hall to ask a knowledgeable party. Matters are resolved more quickly this way than by exchanging e-mail or voice messages. Even the inventor of voice mail, Gordon Matthews, advises users not to hide behind their voice-mail boxes. He encourages them to answer the phone if it rings. But the future doesn't look bright. American parents are already worried about their children's interpersonal skills because they spend more time on the computer than with other children or family members.

In Asia, it is important for a person to be personable. What the Japanese call *ningen-rashi* and Koreans call *eengan-jeokin* is an ability to approach things from a warm, human perspective rather than a cold, robotic one. One puts one's heart in a situation rather than one's head and is warm and generous, nurturing and caring. The Chinese are often reminded that Chin Shih Huang lost his empire because his approach to building the Great Wall was so impersonal. An American businessman living in Singapore said that when he was going to Malaysia for a short business trip, his Asian girlfriend's parents came to the airport to bid him farewell, even though the flight was going to take less than an hour. Asian society may not be as efficient as American, but relationships are certainly more personal.

Overemphasis on Independence

During a vacation to Hawaii, my husband and I noticed an elderly man struggling to push a cartful of groceries. It was hot and humid, and he looked very tired and feeble. I was reminded of my father back in Korea. We cautiously approached the man and politely asked whether he needed any help. He responded rather angrily, "Do I look so weak that I can't care for myself?" An American friend of mine had a similar experience. He went to a two-day business conference, and at the airport he ran into a woman who had attended the same conference. She was petite and was carrying heavy luggage, so he asked whether he could help her. She quite defensively and decisively stated, "I can do it myself." The guiding principle of many Americans is "I'll do my thing, and you do yours."

Although I admire Americans' self-reliance and self-help attitude, their overemphasis on independence causes unnecessary fuss over basic issues, from how to raise a child to how to retire. As soon as my son reached four months of age, people suggested that I move him to his own bedroom. They also suggested that I leave him alone at night and ignore him if he cried. In many families in Asia, young couples can afford only a one-bedroom residence. They don't have the luxury of giving a baby his or her own room, and even if they do, most of them don't want to leave their babies alone. I am not a child development specialist, but it would be interesting to study whether babies learn to be independent in part because they are left alone in their own bedrooms and not given attention when they cry.

My mother worked full-time, but despite her job and her three other children, she tried to breast-feed me as much as possible. She later told me that I wouldn't let her go at night because I had been hungry all day long. Still, I turned out to be very independent compared with most Asians. I chose my own college and major. I decided to come to graduate school in the United States. I supported myself throughout college and graduate school. I traveled to Asia and Europe alone. I chose my spouse. Even when I was young, I was so independent that my parents used to tell me, "Even if we were to leave you alone in a jungle, you would somehow manage to survive."

From an Asian point of view, Americans' individualism is an attempt to deny a natural social structure that exists among humankind. Some people who are obviously in need of help do not ask for it out of fear of being labeled as too dependent. A former professor who was suffering from cancer confessed that his biggest challenge was asking for help. He had been independent all his life. His children had an image of him as an independent man, and he didn't want that to change. I can fully empathize with the man, because I used to be like him. But I came to learn that interdependence could enrich my life in serendipitous ways.

My willingness to depend on others helped me make great friends. I could not afford a car in my early years of graduate school. Being independent, I tried to take city buses and school shuttle buses to go to church, to shop for groceries, or to attend meetings. Gradually, when friends offered me a ride home, I began to take them up on their offers. Occasionally, I invited them to share my humble, homemade Korean meals, which they gladly accepted, giving us more opportunities to develop a friendship. In this way, we slowly became close friends.

Willingness to accept others' help can also benefit those who offer the help. Mary White, a sociologist at Boston University, states that allowing ourselves to be nurtured confers value on the caretaker by giving that person an opportunity to display the valued skill of nurturing. Besides, people who give help become more interested in the people they help. Even within a family, interdependence brings family members closer together, whereas independence can create a sense of self-righteousness and distance. Also, independent people tend to be less sympathetic toward those who need help. In Africa, there is a saying that men become men through other men.

In international business, letting go of pride and asking for help can improve negotiations. One of the mistakes Americans make in negotiating with Asians is that they often present themselves as proud and strong people who can do anything. They act as if they can survive and conquer alone. But if they were willing to let go of some of their independence, they could develop allies instead of enemies. An American lawyer who lived and worked in Japan said that when he shared his worry about specific contract terms and conditions with the Japanese, many of them were more than willing to help him. Another American businessman told about reaching an impasse in a negotiation session with some Korean partners. When the two sides took a break, he said to one of his Korean partners, "You hold my destiny in your hand." And he meant it. After the break, the Korean negotiators were much more gentle and agreeable, and he learned that showing some hurt was his best negotiation strategy.

Admitting that we need help does not mean admitting weakness. Rather it displays the strength to acknowledge that we need the resources around us. As an Asian saying goes, "If you share your happiness, it will be doubled. If you share your unhappiness, it will be halved."

Suing Anybody, Anytime, and Anywhere

Right after President Clinton took office in 1993, I visited with a high-ranking government official from Asia. I asked him what he thought of the Clinton administration. He answered, "The problem with the Clinton administration is that it has too many lawyers. I'm afraid the decisions made by legal-minded people are not the best way to lead a country or to govern people." Certainly, bringing lawyers along is not the best way to build a business relationship in Asia. Asian businessmen are often offended when their American business partners bring lawyers to the negotiating table. It makes them feel that they are not trusted.

With a reputation as the most litigious society in the world, the United States has almost 900,000 lawyers, an average of one lawyer for every 300 people. Some Americans suggest that the U.S. should export lawyers to Asia. The U.S. has 15 times as many lawyers per capita as Japan, 24 times as many as Korea, and 83 times as many as China. It can be argued that easy accessibility to lawyers guarantees Americans equal rights regardless of their background and connections, and to some degree, this is true. In countries with fewer lawyers, most people can't afford a lawyer, and their voices can be ignored in the judicial process. The problem with having too many lawyers is that because they are readily available, people are much less likely to try to settle their disputes directly with the other party. As a result, many Americans do not know how to work out their differences in person any more, and lawyers are eager to take advantage of the situation.

Although Asians have witnessed a significant increase in lawsuits in recent years, they joke about Americans' reliance on lawyers for solving problems: students suing their school boards, employees suing employers, wives suing husbands, children suing parents, patients suing doctors, church members suing pastors, and so on. No matter what kind of relationship they had with the other party, when they feel they have been wronged, Americans are ready to hire a lawyer. For example, Lee Iacocca has sued Chrysler, the very company that he led and turned around so caringly. What was once described as the most beautiful business relationship in the world may now be described as the most disastrous affair of its time. A former Asian personnel manager in the U.S. subsidiary of an Asian company became a legal expert after working in that office for five years. Now he is in charge of an international patent law department, thanks to his experience in dealing with American personnel and lawyers. In Asian companies, human resources managers rarely have to deal with lawyers on personnel issues. They have no need to set aside a budget for legal fees or settlement expenses for employees' lawsuits.

According to an article in the *Wall Street Journal*, 5 February 1998, the surge in malpractice suits leads even pastors to offer less counseling to parishioners. The Christian Legal Society has published tips for clergy who want to avoid liability, including obtaining professional liability insurance for one's counseling ministry. Many Americans blame hungry lawyers for this situation, in which anybody can sue anybody for any reason. Several economists even say that lawyers are ruining the U.S. economy because we all pay the price. Consumers pay higher medical bills because of doctors' high malpractice insurance premiums, and in general, legal fees are built into the price of most products to cover the cost of lawsuits.

But lawyers are not the only ones to blame; everybody plays a role. Compared with Asians, Americans are obsessed with their rights. Many Asian students who come to America prefer to room with other Asian students; they think that Americans assert their rights too much to be able to live in harmony. Americans do not hesitate to say what bothers them but are not as considerate of other parties' interests as Asians are. They are reluctant to compromise on even trivial matters. Many cannot stand any violation of their rights at all.

Conflicts are common in Asia, too, yet most Asians manage to resolve their disputes without going to court. Although bickering and fighting are prevalent, the maintenance of peace and harmonious relations within a community is more important than demanding one's rights. Ordinary people rarely need a lawyer in their lifetime; most things are settled on a personal level. Traditionally, the majority of Asians lived in villages as farmers; a person was born, grew up, married, worked, raised children, grew old, and died in the same village. Thus, people had to learn to live with the others in the community. Many families had known one another for generations. When they had disputes, they relied on intermediaries, not lawyers. The intermediaries, often village leaders, would settle the dispute according to the established custom and the circumstances surrounding the particular case.

Since moving to America, I have been advised to hire lawyers on numerous occasions in which Asians would have settled the matter without them. I have been told that just mentioning a lawyer would help me get my way. Every family I know who has built their own house had to hire a lawyer to resolve conflicts with their contractors. The cost of lawsuits in America is not just monetary. Companies cannot fire unproductive employees for fear of lawsuits. Schools cannot discipline children, and day-care teachers cannot dispense even over-the-counter medicine. For fear of liability, people cannot easily extend help to friends or neighbors. People rarely say "I'm sorry" when there has been an accident, because it could make them appear to be liable in case of a lawsuit. People cannot completely trust one another, even friends.

A German lawyer said, "Most lawsuits are derived from hate. The hate among people is a problem that legal experts cannot solve. It is a very delicate human relationship." Americans say that they seek justice, but in the process, they lose their humanity; instead, cynicism and bitterness prevail. Americans' belief in their law is great, but morality and harmony should be given equal weight in dictating people's behavioral norms. Rules and regulations themselves do not bring justice or humanity. After all, the law was made for people, not the other way around. If Americans would invest more time in developing relationships with the people around them, they would be less likely to sue one another.

Overuse of Warnings and Tips

One German engineer said that U.S. product warnings insult the intelligence of 99 percent of the population in order to warn the other 1 percent. Here are a few examples:

- On a hair dryer: do not use while sleeping
- On a bar of soap: use like regular soap
- On a frozen dinner: serving suggestion—defrost and remove plastic cover
- On a hotel-provided shower cap: fits one head
- On a package of bread pudding: product will be hot after heating
- On an aromatic votive candle: not for consumption

At a seafood restaurant in Maine, I read this warning on the menu: "There may be occasional bones." A sticker on a seedless melon says, "There may be occasional seeds." In a newspaper ad, I read a warning accompanying a coupon: "The company shall not be held responsible for any injuries resulting from using scissors to cut out the coupon." When I bought an organizer for busy women, I found a section on how to hire a housekeeper. Under the subtitle "Advertise in a Newspaper," there was this sample telephone message for a filled position: "Hi! You've reached the Lees. If you're calling about the ad, the position has been filled. Thanks for calling. If you would like to leave a message for the Lees, please do so after the beep." In a California restaurant rest room, I read a sign, "How to lock the door completely." It listed three steps, with the first one being "Close the door all the way." Are these genuine concerns about customers or simply attempts to avoid liability? Although warnings themselves don't free one from the potential for liability, companies or institutions are encouraged by their lawyers to post them anyway.

There is good reason for concern—rampant lawsuits. Two social agencies that run thrift shops with donated items told me that they often have to dispose of waterbeds or playpens for fear that buyers may sue them if there is an accident during use. Despite the warning about tobacco use on each cigarette package, tobacco companies are being sued. This goes against the American philosophy of self-reliance and personal responsibility. Between 1945 and 1999, only 160 product liability cases were tried in Japan. In the United States, I would bet that as many cases are tried on a daily basis. Of course, from a consumer protection point of view, it is wonderful to have a way to fight against a corporate giant if a problem results from the manufacturer's miscalculation or negligence. Still, consumers should take some responsibility for their own negligence.

Warnings are not given just to consumers. In any working relationship, there are warnings. For example, even as an author, I have to sign an indemnity agreement with the publisher. As a consultant and trainer, I also sign indemnity agreements plus nondisclosure agreements with my clients. Once I made travel arrangements through a high-tech firm's travel agency. Since I was flying for the company, I was able to get its corporate rate for my airfare. But I also had to fill out a legal document that said that I would not reveal the special rate to any outsider because the fare was company proprietary information. Most celebrities require their assistants, nannies, domestic help, or even lovers to sign nondisclosure agreements.

Because of warnings, directions for using American

products are much longer than for products from other countries. For a tea bag made in Asia, for instance, the instructions simply say, "Pour hot water. May want to add sugar or honey." On a box of American tea, there are more directions, including "Start with clean water." (Is there anyone who starts with dirty water?) For packaged food, directions often include such useless tips as "Freeze the rest for future use" and "Reheat in skillet until it's hot." Suppose you wish to serve it cold? Directions for baking a frozen pie advise you to "take the pie out of the box." I once compared American and Japanese cooking-oil bottles. An American bottle has a warning "in case there is a fire." American packages contain a lot of information that is beyond consumers' interest, and manufacturers kindly provide toll-free phone numbers for any other questions. On a package of peanuts given on Southwest Airlines, I read, "Please call 1-800 number for nutrition information."

Americans also have manuals for everything, and most of them include too many directions and suggestions. When I was working for a major American management consulting company, I used to write instructors' manuals for the client firm's training programs. These manuals had to include every single phrase and gesture to be used by an instructor, including "Welcome students (with smile)." On the positive side, this ensures consistency in the quality of training regardless of the instructor, but it may also be why many American consultants have a reputation for suggesting the obvious.

Numerous how-to books and magazine articles also insult the intelligence of average people. Once I read a book on the executive image, written by a well-known authority.

Included in the book was a chapter on how to take care of one's clothing and how to read sewn-in labels. The author went on to explain that "machine wash" means "use automatic washer" and that "small load" means "smaller than normal washload." To my surprise, she didn't clarify what a normal washload was. I guess it's a good thing to be warned of any serious danger involved in using a product or service, for one person's common sense may not be as good as another's. But the more useless warning signs we see, the more likely we are to ignore them—and the more likely we are to ignore the important ones.

Families at Risk

If there were a fire at home, what possessions would you want to save first? Most Americans would say photographs. This perplexes a lot of Asians, because most of them would try to save things like wedding rings, money, gold, antiques, and other items of monetary value. But strangely, although Americans cherish their memories, they don't seem to value the institution that creates such memories and pictures.

According to Confucius, everything in life stems from five basic relationships: father to son, sovereign to subject, husband to wife, elder to younger, and friend to friend. Asians believe that when the basic relationships are in working order, there is peace in the world. While Americans often espouse human rights abroad, they seem to ignore the conflict that exists within their own families. I am often asked about the divorce rate in Korea. It was 2.3 per 1,000 couples in 1994. True, not all Asian couples are happy. In a poll of married couples in Japan, for instance, fewer than half of the respondents said that they would marry the same person if given the chance to do it over again, and some Asian couples stay married without much excitement or romance in their relationship. Yet many Asians believe in *jeong* (emotional attachment strengthened over time), which becomes a stronger bond than romantic love for couples. They do not get married at the peak of their love and go downhill thereafter, as many Americans appear to do. They develop a greater attachment the longer they live together. They don't go into marriage saying, "If it doesn't work out, I can always quit."

Buddhists emphasize *yin-yeon*: some people are destined to meet each other. According to Buddhism, two people meet in the present life because of connections they made in their previous lives. If two people have jobs in the same workplace, it is because of yin-yeon; even accidentally touching someone's sleeve on the street is caused by yin-yeon. Although a person has many yin-yeon connections in a lifetime, their degree of intensity varies. Considering all the people one can meet in one's many lives, the chance of a person meeting his or her current mate occurs only once every three hundred years—all the more reason to honor that connection and strengthen it over time.

Despite this belief, divorce rates have been steadily increasing in Asian countries. As women achieve more economic independence, they are more willing to leave their husbands when faced with adversity. When couples feel that they have made wrong choices, they go their separate ways. Nevertheless, when couples have children, they seriously consider their decision to separate. Asians tend to view their children, rather than each other, as the primary focus of their marriage. Couples stay together to provide stability for their children. For a long time, even the language reflected the concept of two parents. When I learned English in Korea, I was told that the word *parents* should always be used in the plural, never the singular. In Korean culture, having only one parent was abnormal.

Asian parents would rather sacrifice their own happiness than make their children suffer because of a divorce. They compare rearing children to planting seeds, which they expect to harvest in the autumn of their lives. Interestingly, couples who are unhappy with each other in their early years often seem to get along well later on. They come to realize that love takes sacrifice.

It is unfortunate that many Americans are no longer prepared to work to save a marriage or even take responsibility for their children. They believe that not loving each other is reason enough to divorce. For people who don't have children, that may be enough. But if couples have children, they should make every effort to save their marriages. Allan Bloom wrote in *The Closing of the American Mind*, "To children, the voluntary separation of parents seems worse than their death precisely because it is voluntary. The important lesson that the family taught was the existence of the only unbreakable bond, for better or for worse, between human beings."

The family is the basic unit of society and is at the heart of its survival. Families give stability to society. Even if governments disappear, families survive. Almost two-thirds of rapists, three-quarters of adolescent murderers, and three-quarters of long-term prison inmates are young men who grew up without fathers in the house. When a father is present in the household, teenage girls get pregnant 50 percent less frequently than their fatherless counterparts. Children in a mother-father household are less likely to drop out of school, get involved with drugs, be delinquent, or suffer child abuse.

No one can deny that some couples are unhappy with each other; not all marriages are made in heaven. When I was growing up, I often wondered how my own parents chose each other. My mother was an idealist, and my father was a pragmatist. Mom was adventuresome, and Dad was a homebody. They seemed to have completely different perceptions of life. To make matters worse, they had to face a financial crisis when one of my mother's relatives ran away with my father's pension funds. Suddenly, they had no savings and four daughters to educate. In a country where education loans were not easily available, they were financially strained. They constantly fought, and whenever they argued, my mom said that the only reason she was staying in the marriage was because she didn't want to give her daughters the stigma of being children of divorce. Now that we are adults, we four daughters are grateful to our parents for staying married, and my parents are happy that they stayed together. They have told me that now that all the children are grown, there is no reason to fight. They are devoted to each other.

Like many Asian couples, my parents believed in saving their marriage because of their children, and they worked out their differences. In time, problems can usually be worked out, as long as the two partners try to resolve them earnestly and honestly. Couples don't have to pretend to have a perfect marriage when they don't. Rather, it is important to have a realistic expectation of marriage and to teach children how to resolve conflicts with patience. Unfortunately, many American families give up too quickly and rely on lawyers to settle their disputes. According to *USA Today*, in 1999, the top six categories in a search on lawyers.com (which lists 420,000 lawyers) were family, 36 percent; criminal, 16 percent; employment, 15 percent; personal injury, 12 percent; real estate, 12 percent; and business, 9 percent.

The family must be a place where a child can learn about tolerating differences and valuing diversity in a larger world. Compared with Asians, Americans have far more help in dealing with interpersonal matters, including books, videos, and Websites on how to improve relationships, revive a marriage, handle in-laws, manage a tough boss, deal with difficult people, and so on. But obviously, these tools are not keeping Americans' relationships happy and healthy.

Many Americans are concerned about whether their children will have the same standard of living they have enjoyed. But they should be more concerned about what kind of society they are leaving for their children. Those who are concerned about human rights and peace in other countries would do well to first ensure love and peace in their own homes and within their own families. The family should be the first place where children learn about healthy human relationships. From the family, children learn loyalty and a sense of order; from their parents, they learn that love takes sacrifice.

It is important to note that three of Confucius' five basic relationships involve the family. An Asian saying goes:

"First, a man must cultivate himself; second, he must manage his home; third, he must govern the country; then there will be peace on earth."

Insufficient Emphasis on Filial Piety

There is an American children's storybook titled *The Runaway Bunny*. It tells of a mother's steadfast commitment to stay near her child wherever he or she goes. In the story, a little bunny tells his mother, "I am running away." "If you run away, I will run after you," says his mother. "Then I will be a fish and swim away from you." The mother says, "I will become a fisherman to catch you." The young bunny continues, "Then I will become a rock on the mountain, high above you." The mother says, "Then I will be a mountain climber." The story continues with the little bunny imagining other scenarios that will allow him to run away from the care of his mother, until he finally concedes, "Shucks, I might just as well stay where I am."

Compare this story with an Asian children's story. Once there was a little frog. He was very naughty and did the exact opposite of what his mother told him to do. If his mother told him not to go outside, he would go out without telling her. If his mother told him not to go near dangerous creatures, he would go as far as he could. If his mother told him not to eat more than two cookies, he would clean out the jar. Finally, his mother got very sick. She knew that she would die soon. She wanted to be buried on the top of a great mountain. Since her son had always done the opposite of what she had asked, she summoned him and requested that he bury her near the river, thinking that he would bury her on the mountain. After she died, the little frog was so sad that for the first time he decided to grant her wish. He buried her near the water, but every time it rained, he was afraid that his mother's grave would be washed away. The story concludes: that is why frogs cry hard on rainy days.

In reading the bunny story, American children may be profoundly comforted by this loving, dedicated mother who promises to find her child every time he threatens to run away. It assures little children of their mothers' never-ending, unconditional love. It does not, however, teach what a child should do to return the mother's love. In contrast, through the story of the disobedient but regretful frog, Asian children are reminded to obey and serve their parents well while they are alive.

Compared with Asian countries, the United States teaches very little about concern and respect for one's parents. I have yet to see a book on American values or virtues that includes filial piety. In fact, most Americans have never heard of the term. Of course, Christian Americans have been reminded of one aspect of filial piety through the Ten Commandments: honor thy parents. Jewish Americans are also taught to respect elders. Most of the rest express their love and gratitude to their parents on Mother's Day and Father's Day. Other than that, there is scant emphasis on filial piety. Through storytelling, Asian children learn about the importance of honoring their parents from early childhood. Children are advised to express gratitude to their parents while they can, because one is never certain how long one's parents will remain in this world. At school, Asian children read stories of exemplary sons and daughters who care for their parents through good times and bad.

Throughout history, Asians have been deeply influenced by the concept of filial piety. This emphasis started even before Confucius began to preach its virtue. At the beginning of the Chou dynasty in China, around 1122 B.C., filial piety was not merely a moral but also a legal obligation. A son who didn't serve his father respectfully was regarded as a criminal and was subject to merciless punishment. Later, in the *Book of Rites*, Tseng Tzu stated, "There are three kinds of filial piety: the highest form of filial piety is to honor your parents; the next one, not to humiliate them; the next, to feed them." Honoring parents is something that Asians take seriously. Asian children want their parents to be proud of them. Among Asian American students in the United States, there is a joke about how to be a perfect child. One way is to get all A-pluses and to be admitted to and receive scholarship offers from all the Ivy League schools.

Taking care of elderly parents is another important aspect of filial piety. However, even in Asia, caring for elderly parents is becoming less popular—younger generations prefer to be responsible for only their nuclear families and don't want to give their parents the care they need. In a recent poll conducted in China, 75 percent of respondents said that they would be reluctant to have their parents live with them. Thus, affluent elders are considering other options, such as nursing homes. In fact, some Asians argue that their tradition of filial piety imposes too heavy a burden on their children and that they must develop a social system like that in the United States to take care of elders. Nevertheless, sending parents to nursing homes is still considered inhumane; Asians feel responsible for their parents.

Filial piety does not, however, mean unconditional obedience to parents. Confucius said, "A pious son will obey his father's orders without idleness, gently admonish his parents with perseverance, and labor for his parents without complaint." Indeed, some parents in Asia can be unreasonable in their demands and cause their children great unhappiness. In that situation, children are encouraged to gently correct their parents.

In a way, American parents and children can have healthier relationships than their Asian counterparts if both are self-sufficient. There is a beauty in the American philosophy of parenting: if you love your children, set them free. Like the mother in *The Runaway Bunny*, many American parents do an excellent job of giving their children love without expecting anything in return. They have wonderful relationships with their children. At the same time, there are cultural and social factors that are not conducive to making filial piety an American value. Due to an overemphasis on independence and self-reliance, Americans believe that all adults should take care of themselves. Because everyone is self-made, many feel that they don't owe their success to their parents. Stressing individual rights and happiness also encourages some parents to pursue their own happiness rather than sacrifice for their family's sake. When children grow up in such an environment, it is difficult for them to make sacrifices for their parents. America's vast size and Americans' busy lifestyle don't help the family either. As Americans move around in the land of opportunity, it is challenging for them to care for their parents hundreds of miles away. When dual-career couples barely have time for their own lives, they have little left for their parents. Furthermore, having a few sets of stepparents makes filial piety an almost impossible goal to achieve.

I admire those Americans who are selflessly taking care of their elderly parents. Even in Asia, that is becoming a noble example for children. But for those who don't feel the obligation or the need to take care of their aging parents, the least they can do is show a sense of gratitude. It is so sad to see people blaming their parents for everything that is wrong in their lives. Emotionally closed people blame their parents for never hugging them or not saying "I love you." People with low self-esteem criticize their parents for comparing them with other children or being overly critical of them. Adult children of divorce attribute their own marital unhappiness to their parents' divorce. Some obese people even blame their mothers for not teaching them how to eat right.

Asian children rarely blame their parents openly. When they feel like blaming their parents, they remember the sacrifices their parents made. People say that only after one becomes a parent can one appreciate the hearts of parents. I know that appreciating my parents means accepting my responsibility to take care of them when they need me and passing down their love to my son.

Poor Basic Education

A Harvard student was standing in line at an express checkout in a grocery store near Cambridge. In front of him was a young man with twelve items, although the sign clearly said ten items or fewer. The checkout clerk asked him, "Are you an MIT student who can't read or a Harvard student who can't count?" The store clerk had a wry sense of humor, but unfortunately, it reflects the reality of a country that has tumbled to the bottom of the heap among industrialized countries in basic education.

A few years ago, *Business Week* reported that employers had found that 21 percent of high school graduates could barely read a training manual, and 50 percent could not communicate very well through writing. Twenty-seven percent of high school seniors did not have good basic math skills; one-third couldn't compute the price of a $1,250 stereo that was on sale for 20 percent off.

I heard a story about a hamburger shop that learned by experience about the deplorable state of Americans' math competency. It advertised a special promotion serving one-third-pound hamburgers instead of quarter-pound burgers, and the sales actually declined. Later, store managers found out that many customers thought one-third was smaller than one-quarter. I have seen customers waiting patiently at stores when computer systems are down, because most cashiers are completely lost without them. For math-challenged customers, some restaurants post tipping charts, and retail stores offering 40 percent off display calculated sale prices.

Professionals or highly educated people are not necessarily better off when it comes to math or spelling. Americans laughed at former vice president Dan Quayle for misspelling the word *potato*, but I wonder what the results would be if a basic math quiz were given to politicians. It is puzzling that although America has a passion for quantification—from the tallest buildings to the fat content of foods—its people are challenged in doing simple math.

Once Ann Landers reprinted the actual questions asked
of a witness by a lawyer during a trial. It was originally
published in the Massachusetts Bar Association magazine.

Q: She had three children, right?

A: Yes.

Q: How many were boys?

A: None.

Q: Were there any girls?

Some Americans may say, "Don't worry. We are still the
number-one country in the world." Americans are proud of
their technological prowess, but most don't realize that a lot
of that American talent comes from people who received
their basic education in other countries. In 1980, about a
fifth of the scientists in America (those with doctorates)
were from abroad. Over the subsequent decade, 60 percent
of the American-based authors whose papers in the physical
sciences were most frequently cited were foreign born, as
were nearly 30 percent of the authors of the most-cited
papers in life science. Almost a quarter of the founders or
chairmen of biotechnology companies that went public in
the early 1990s were also originally from other countries.
Yes, the United States is known for having the best higher
education system in the world, but what about those Americans who don't have an opportunity to pursue higher
education? Shouldn't the public school system guarantee
better basic education for them?

There are various theories about the reasons for poor
educational performance in the United States. One reason is
large class size, about 22 to 25 students per class, and even 30
or more in some districts. As a mother of a child in school, I
prefer a small class (13 to 17 students) and see its benefit.

Large classes, however, cannot be an excuse for poor performance. In Korea, Singapore, Japan, and Taiwan, where children have the highest recorded math scores, the class size is often 35 or more and sometimes up to 50. Some argue that children fail because of factors beyond their teachers' control, such as poverty or deteriorating families. Yet other countries have many fewer resources to educate their children. According to data from the Organization for Economic Cooperation and Development, U.S. schools were the least efficient in the industrial world; the U.S. spent more per pupil than almost any other nation, yet its year-to-year gains in student academic achievement were among the smallest. American students made just 78 percent of the progress of students in 15 other countries.

Perhaps one reason that American children don't receive good basic education is because they spend so much time on sports and extracurricular activities. In addition, they spend too much time participating in social activities and thinking about the opposite sex. In most Asian countries, teens have less pressure to perform socially. If there is any pressure, it is to avoid engaging in sex until they graduate from high school or even college. They are too busy with school. The average length of a school year in Japan is 243 days, compared with 180 days in America. Sixteen-hour days are routine for many schoolchildren in China, Japan, and Korea. After a long school day, Asian students typically attend after-school lessons. They spend more than two hours per day on homework, compared with twenty-five minutes in America.

I know many American parents are trying to see that their children get a good education. Parents even try to combine math education with having fun and receiving prizes. Some even hire professionals who can teach math in a fun way at birthday parties. But the success of learning should not be measured by the degree of fun. Sometimes children have to learn to stay the course even though it's not fun.

Inability to Speak Foreign Languages

"If you speak three languages, you are called multilingual. If you speak two languages, you are called bilingual. So what do people call you if you speak only one language? An American." Americans often joke about their inability to speak foreign languages. An American consultant at a prestigious management consulting firm experienced frustration at her firm's worldwide managers' meetings. Most of the Europeans there were able to communicate with one another, but she couldn't understand a thing.

Given a chance, children are capable of learning many languages. Most Dutch people speak three or four languages. Singapore has four official languages, and all students are required to study English in addition to their native language. Although 70 percent of the population is Chinese, education and business are conducted in English. With a country slogan of "Unity in diversity," Singapaore does well with its multiple languages and still manages to be one of the most economically competitive nations in the world. Korea, Japan, Taiwan, and other countries also require English from seventh grade or earlier. During their high school years, many students are required to take a second foreign language. Some parents are willing to provide additional private language lessons.

Their lack of foreign language skills limits Americans' appreciation of other cultures and even alienates them from other nations. One Harris poll asked, "If cost were not an issue, what would your dream vacation spot be?" The top six spots were Australia, Great Britain, Germany, Italy, France, and Canada (in order of preference). It is interesting that three are English-speaking countries, including the top two.

To give American youth new possibilities for world-class leadership, Americans should encourage them to study foreign languages seriously. Although English is a de facto business language, still only one out of every six people in the world speaks it. In international business, the motto is, "I sell in your language, and I buy in my language." With their inability to speak at least one major foreign language, Americans are losing potential business opportunities.

According to a *Wall Street Journal* article, affluent parents in New York are now sending their children to foreign language centers. Madonna is planning to send her daughter, Lourdes, to an exclusive French school in England. Madonna is fluent in Italian and very good at French and Spanish. She has found her languages invaluable. For example, when she was selected for the role of Eva Perón in the movie *Evita*, she was instrumental in getting permission from the president of Argentina to use the palace for the movie. What language did she use to speak to the president? Spanish.

The opportunity to learn another language should not, however, be limited to children of the rich. My parents gave me that opportunity when they were living from paycheck to paycheck. They sent me to a foreign language institute when I was in the third grade. Even though Korea's per capita GNP was only one hundred dollars at the time, my parents foresaw globalization and the need for foreign language skills. Thanks to their encouragement, I took English, German, French, and Japanese; now I want to learn Spanish also.

With the changing global marketplace, America more than ever needs people who have cross-cultural knowledge and transnational skills that will help them work effectively with those from different cultures. With competition coming from all over the world, the days are over when America could economically overpower other countries by doing business "the American way." Despite their huge success in marketing American culture abroad, if U.S. companies want to continue to dominate certain markets, they need people who know more about local culture and history. As David Simon, former chairman of British Petroleum, commented on its operation in seventy markets around the world, "Knowing some of the culture and the political background is half way, if not more than half way, to getting the solution."

If Americans remain reluctant to learn foreign languages and cultures, they will lose major sectors of the world market to multilingual countries and companies that know how to adapt to local cultures. Since English has become practically a universal language, most Americans assume that they will never have to master or even be conversant in a foreign language. That may be true, but they are at a distinct disadvantage compared with their counterparts from other countries who are fluent in at least one foreign language and often two or three. By learning a

foreign language, Americans will not only earn more respect and increase their business clout; they will also
develop compassion for those who have to speak English as
a second or a foreign language.

Lack of Character Education

"My conscience is clean. I don't use it," reads a bumper
sticker on a car parked on a university campus. According
to Hitler's own words, he was without conscience; he called
conscience a Jewish invention. Many Americans deplore
that America has lost its sense of right and wrong. They are
concerned that if this social trend continues, their children
will not be able to find decent mates and have close-knit
families of their own.

In a recent study on peer power, author Patricia Adler
concluded that by late elementary school, boys understand
that their popularity depends on toughness, troublemaking,
domination, coolness, and interpersonal bragging and spar-
ring skills. Girls derive status from success at grooming,
clothes, and other appearance-related variables. It seems
that schools or families don't have enough power to counter
peer pressure and to offer guidance to American youth.

The Chinese symbol for education has two characters—
the first meaning to impart, and the second to develop. The
goal of education is to produce citizens who are balanced in
their pursuit of knowledge, character, and physical fitness.
Due to an American culture that worships sports heroes and
Hollywood celebrities, American children's lives are overly
skewed toward a physical orientation. Most sports programs
are supposed to promote the old virtues—self-confidence,

personal responsibility, teamwork, persistence, and the ability to win and lose with grace. Yet children need to have a balanced education and invest their time and energy in developing their minds and their characters.

In many Asian countries, ethics and moral studies are part of the school curriculum from the first grade. In class, students learn what it means to be genuine human beings and what responsibilities they have as social beings. They learn that their individual actions have social consequences and that they have duties to others. They receive weekly moral education, and teachers assess their character at the end of each semester. In addition, they are required to take music, fine arts, and foreign languages throughout high school, and these broaden their perspective.

Yet character education is not only the job of the schools. Character building begins at home, and parents need to set high expectations and rules for their children. One thing I find interesting in American children's communication is that they don't apologize in situations that seem to warrant it. On such occasions, I have heard children say, "I didn't mean it. It was an accident." Some parents are reluctant to teach children to apologize, maybe because they think that self-esteem means never having to say, "I'm sorry." In contrast, in Japan, *sorry* is one of the few words that mothers make a fuss about having a child say when the child is judged to have offended. According to Joy Hardy, author of *Becoming Japanese: The World of the Pre-school Child*, harmony among children is an important ideal from a very early age, and the word *sorry* and its acceptance enable a tense situation to be restored to harmony.

In addition, Asians believe in the use of shame. Shame

is a controversial concept in America, but in Asia, it is a necessary human characteristic. According to an Asian sage, two characteristics of humans, as distinct from the lower animals, are *kyung* and *chi*. *Kyung* is respect, and *chi* is shame. Respect can develop into faith, and shame can develop into morality. With kyung, people feel a sense of awe toward the divine and believe in divine judgment, which decrees that the righteous always prevail. With chi, they avoid doing wrong. Shame and dishonor protect people.

Some American day-care teachers have told me that they are reluctant to give children a time-out or any punishment for aggressive behavior because the offenders might lose self-esteem. I wonder whether such reinforcement produces children who steal from someone's locker for fun or who shoot their classmates without feeling any guilt. As much as I believe in the power of self-esteem, I also feel just as strongly that children must be taught to tell right from wrong and to be ashamed of doing wrong. Not every shame is "toxic" shame that makes one feel responsible for everything that has gone wrong. Americans constantly remind their children how special they are, but teaching children to feel good regardless of their actions does not do anyone any good.

I often wonder why American schools and society have such a hard time dealing with youth when most parents say, "I'm so lucky. My kids are very good." In a survey of three thousand adults, most respondents didn't believe that today's children would grow up to make the world a better place. However, they excluded their own children from that negative judgment. There is an enormous discrepancy between how good Americans think their own children are and how bad they think others' children are.

If parents are really concerned about their children's future, they have to ensure that their children are choosing friends with a sense of morality (ethical standards). It's not good enough to raise positive children in a negative world. Parents have to make their children's world a positive place where they will learn good values. There is a story in Asia that is used to emphasize the importance of the environment in the development of character. When Mencius, a great Chinese philosopher, was a little boy, he lost his father. His single mother was determined to give her son a good education so that he would not be labeled as a "fatherless boy" who didn't learn right from wrong. They happened to live near a cemetery. One day, the mother saw little Mencius imitating the workers digging the graves. She didn't think that grave diggers were good role models, so she moved to a house near a marketplace. When he began to imitate merchants selling and bartering for items, she didn't approve of this either. Finally, she moved next to a learning center. Only then, when he was imitating children reading and studying, did she feel that she had provided the right environment.

Parents must realize that teaching character requires time and patience. I am appalled at the number of American children diagnosed with attention deficit disorder (10 percent) and at the use of the behavior-altering drug Ritalin—the United States uses 90 percent of the world supply. I am sure that some children benefit from the drug, but I share the concern of other educators who say that some parents use it because discipline is more time-consuming and taxing than popping a pill.

"All kids are our kids," says Dr. Peter Benson, president of the Search Institute, which was founded in 1958 to advance the well-being of children. It is our responsibility as adults to ensure that all children are exposed to more honesty, family life and values, morals, respect, fidelity, kindness, tolerance for others, decency, and trust in their communities, either real or virtual. Unlike in collective cultures, teaching moral values is not an easy task in America, because Americans do not always agree on whose values should be adopted. However, it is important to remember that society cannot be sustained when its constituents do not know right from wrong, do not share common values, and do not instill those values in their children. Despite cultural relativity, there are universal virtues that elevate humanity and make life meaningful.

Disrespect for Teachers

Whenever I conduct corporate training sessions in America, I can't help thinking that in Asia, I'm a respected teacher, but in the United States, I'm just a humble vendor. A few years ago, I gave a one-day seminar to the top-level executives of a major Korean corporation. After the morning session, I went to the rest room to wash my hands. When I came back to the room where lunch was being served, everybody was standing, including the president of the company, who looked about my father's age. Surprised, I asked why they were standing. The president answered, "Today you're the teacher, so we cannot sit down before you are seated."

Traditionally in Asia, there were four classes: *sa* (scholars), *nong* (farmers), *kong* (technicians), and *sang* (merchants). Given Asians' traditional emphasis on education, teachers were the highest class and enjoyed the most prestige.

In Asia, teaching was considered a calling from heaven. Confucius regarded teaching a good student as one of the greatest joys in life. In traditional China, teachers were held in such high regard that they were considered one of the five entities worthy of worship; the others were heaven, earth, emperor, and parents. Students were even prohibited from stepping on the shadows of teachers. Although teaching has lost some of its former esteem in modern Asia, respect for teachers is still shown in various ways. Even today, many Asians use the term *teacher* as a courteous form of address equivalent to the American "Mr." and "Mrs." When Asians pay teachers, they put the money in an envelope; it is considered crude to present checks or cash without an envelope. Asians ensure that they convey their respect and care for their teachers. One American who taught English in a Japanese middle school said that every day at lunchtime, Japanese students brought a Big Mac to his desk. They thought that he missed his American diet. In Korea, schools celebrate and recognize Teacher's Day, when ceremonies are held at schools to honor teachers. From kindergarten to graduate school, students and parents bring flowers or gifts to teachers to express their gratitude. The president honors model teachers and the media report stories of exemplary teachers. On holidays, it's common for former students to visit their teachers and take them out to lunch or dinner.

Due to this cultural influence, I could not bring myself to call my professors by their first names during my U.S. graduate school years, even though other American students did so. Even now, I am told, Asians who come to

American corporations for training have a hard time calling their instructors by their first names. They would rather call them "Teacher" or "Sir" to show respect. Influenced by this tradition, an American teacher of Chinese descent refused to call her principal by his first name in front of her students. She said, "I would like to set an example for my students. Calling you by your first name will not help that."

Confucius' emphasis on learning and the veneration of teachers account for the high value that the Chinese, Japanese, Koreans, and Vietnamese place on education. Educational credentials are very important for career advancement in those countries, and both parents and students regard education as the highest priority. This creates a learning environment that is more disciplined than that of the United States. It is not uncommon for Asian parents to ask teachers to be tougher on their children so that they will spend more time studying. Also, Asian teachers are given greater authority than their American counterparts in disciplining students. Many Americans who have taught Asian students say that they enjoy teaching them because their parents are much more supportive of a disciplined school system.

In America, teachers are perceived as people who have knowledge about certain subjects, but they are not necessarily respected figures with authority. Some parents and students even see themselves as consumers—buying an education from teachers—and blame the teachers for low grades. A comparative study of five hundred parents in the United States and Japan asked them why their children did not do well in school. Most American parents blamed teachers, whereas the Japanese blamed themselves.

American parents also blame large class sizes, but the real problem is their unwillingness to give teachers respect and authority in the classroom. In fact, classes in America are generally smaller than those in Asia. Yet most Asian children are better mannered and more orderly in class than American students, because teachers can take disciplinary action. Most American parents object to corporal punishment; teachers who use strict discipline are not popular. Yet parents also expect teachers to play the role of classroom enforcers; many teachers are so busy maintaining class order that they have time for little else. Numerous teachers have told me that they are simply burned out. As a result, smart young people are discouraged from pursuing the profession; a teaching career will not reward them financially or psychologically.

In contrast, Americans are willing to pay millions of dollars to athletes and coaches. Some say that this trend has produced a situation in which two people are qualified to teach calculus and five are qualified to teach football. In fact, football coaches are paid much more than classroom teachers and sometimes even college presidents.

Unfortunately, even in Asia, the teaching profession is not as respected as it was in the past. In Japan and Korea, recent violence against teachers has shocked both societies. However, most Asian parents still do not challenge the authority of teachers, nor would they sue the school system over a teacher's taking disciplinary actions.

The Asian way of honoring teachers can have a negative impact on society, too. Teachers are only human, and some teachers show favoritism to students whose parents give them money or gifts. Some teachers also misuse their authority and abuse students, using unnecessarily harsh punishment or touching students inappropriately. I must admit that when I recall my school days, there are some disciplinary actions I would not want a teacher to exercise on any child. Nevertheless, American parents should give teachers due respect and authority so that they can focus on teaching. And teachers should conduct themselves properly, so that they can become professionals worthy of society's trust, respect, and praise.

Talking Too Much

"Don't be afraid to speak up, or you may be considered dumb." A mentor who had been educated in the United States told me this as I was preparing to come to graduate school in America. Upon arrival, I quickly realized that I would be quite invisible unless I spoke up, because everyone else was talking.

From an early age, Americans are encouraged to talk whenever they wish. American parents tend to respect children's opinions and encourage them to express themselves verbally. Schools encourage debates and reward verbal skills. This environment has created people who love to talk and are not afraid to say what they think. Americans' passion for talk is reflected in its number of radio and television talk shows, including a twenty-four-hour talk-show station. No fewer than twenty-five television talk shows vie for America's attention, from Oprah to Geraldo, Montel to Maury, Rosie to Ricki, Jerry to Jenny. Guests are ready to talk about almost anything, including their sex lives, shopping secrets, baby or pet care, politics, and fashion. In fact, many Americans find that even with all this talking they have too little opportunity to express their opinions. Thus, they have other outlets as well. Americans lose sleep to chat on the Internet. They let others know their beliefs through bumper stickers, T-shirts, license plates, posters, and mugs.

The problem is that cheap talk has become the norm, and people simply do not take the time to filter their thoughts before mass-distributing them. Too many people talk without thinking clearly. Asian businesspeople complain that Americans talk a lot but rarely make a point. When people like to hear themselves, they rarely listen. When they listen, they don't listen attentively. According to a study of people's listening habits, Americans' listening efficiency is a mere 25 percent.

In Asia, words are not so cheap. From childhood, Asians quickly learn the importance of reticence, modesty, indirection, and humility: a person should be quiet unless he is absolutely confident about what he has to say. They learn *nam-ah-il-eon-joong-cheon-geum*, which in Korean means that a man's word should be equal to tons of gold. Men are expected to speak prudently and succinctly, with the intention of keeping their word. It is more acceptable for women to be talkative, but even for women, too much talking is considered a vice. Traditionally, a man of character speaks less and a man of no character speaks more. Great scholars and philosophers, especially, are supposed to refrain from commenting on history or people. Some Zen Buddhists were taught that the overuse of one's tongue could damage one's heart. I don't know whether there is any scientific evidence supporting this belief, but I prefer not to take the risk.

In America, people have strong opinions about everything and are not afraid to express them. When I interviewed an executive of a major American company, he said that he never lacked an opinion. In working with senior executives in Asia, I never met anyone who could say that. In a way, I appreciate Americans' talking straight, because I never have to guess their true intentions. The Japanese are known for their particular brand of doublespeak: *honne* is surface communication, and *tatemae* represents real intentions. Other Asians can also be vague, tentative, and indirect, which makes it difficult for outsiders to read their intentions.

Americans pay a price for always being ready to talk: they often reveal themselves imprudently. Once I was sitting in a customer lounge at a car service center along with a gentleman in his sixties. We got into a conversation, and within fifteen minutes, he had told me about his two marriages, his children, and his various properties in several states. I had not asked for any of that. In Asia, people do not reveal their personal lives so quickly; only those in one's inner circle are supposed to know the intimate details of one's life. Sharing one's personal history or life story with a stranger may not be so costly, but excessive talking can be very expensive. Valuable technologies can be leaked to other companies or countries by technologists bragging (at a bar or trade show) about what they are developing. As a former student of technology transfer, I have learned that human communication is one of the most important carriers.

Many Americans simply cannot stand silence; they will say anything to fill it. However, silence can be communication too. We cannot *not* communicate. In Japan, eloquence is often nonverbal. It is said that the Japanese have cultivated their silence and intuitive communication because of their traditional homes: small rooms and paper walls. Koreans' indirect communication is partly due to ethnic homogeneity. Because 99 percent of the population is ethnic Korean, there is an intuitive understanding and thus no need for a great deal of articulation. In general, Asians assume *ishim jeonshim* (the Japanese call it *ishin denshin*) in their communication, which means, "If it is in one's heart, it will be transmitted to another's heart." Since what one is thinking can be communicated without the medium of words, Asians believe that it is unnecessary to verbalize everything. Sentences are left unfinished so that the other person can conclude them in his or her own mind. In Japanese business, the motto is "Hear one, understand ten." Although this practice can sometimes cause confusion and frustration, Asians are more prudent and sincere when they do decide to speak.

To be taken seriously, Americans should go on a "talking diet"—take the time to digest a situation and weigh the impact of their words on other people. In front of many Japanese Shinto shrines, there are water fountains. Before entering the shrines, people rinse their mouths to cleanse themselves of their sins; it is a symbolic gesture before presenting themselves to God, for they have sinned with their tongues. At a Buddhist retreat in Thailand, participants are required to keep silent for a week. This would not be very popular among Americans, but for those who pursue virtue, occasional abstinence from talking can be worthwhile. Americans who hurry to talk must reflect on what Lao Tzu said: "Those who know do not speak. Those who speak do not know."

Exaggeration and Overconfidence

An Asian manager who had been working in the United States for three months complained about Americans' confidence. "Whenever I ask my American staff whether they can do something, the answer is always yes," he said. He inquisitively added, "How come Americans say 'no problem' all the time when I see problems everywhere?" Other non-American managers working in the U.S. have also observed a tremendous gap between American job candidates' self-described abilities and their real job competencies. Influenced by their marketing culture, Americans oversell themselves on their resumés or in interviews, exaggerating their experiences and capabilities.

Although positive thinking and positive talking have merit, many Americans' expressions are too optimistic and unrealistic. Some people always say "Never better" when asked how they are doing. One Asian businessman asked why Americans say "Great" when asked "How are you?" He said, "When I learned English in my country, I was told that there are at least two responses to 'How are you?'—'So-so' and 'Great.' But since I came to the U.S., I've never met anyone who said 'So-so.'" Employees who have been laid off often complain that only weeks before their layoffs they had been praised for their performance.

Celebrities seem to depict some of the worst examples of exaggeration. Whenever they marry (which is quite often), they say, "I've found the love of my life" or "I have never been happier" or "He is my soul mate" or "This is a marriage made in heaven." In a short time they file for divorce because of "irreconcilable differences." Ordinary people play their own parts in exaggeration. When I said to an acquaintance at her wedding, "I hope you will be happy a long, long time," she cheerfully responded, "Absolutely. There is no doubt about that." If I had said that to an Asian friend, a likely response would have been, "I don't know. I will do my best" or "I hope so, too." In Asia, many couples get married through match-makers, and occasionally the interval between the first meeting and the wedding is only a month. When a bride is asked whether she loves the groom, she is likely to confess, "I like him all right, but it's too soon to know whether it is love." Even if one is sure, the answer should not sound so certain. In Asia, humbleness is a virtue, and modesty is a sign of good character. Japanese conversation is full of such words and phrases as "Maybe," "I think it's possible," and "I'm not really sure."

Even if I envy Americans' enthusiasm for life and optimism about the future, their common use of such superlatives as *superb, phenomenal, great, fantastic,* and *excellent* in daily conversation is a reflection of overstimula-tion and overdramatization. People are not impressed with modest words any more; situations must be exaggerated to get someone's attention. Advertisements are full of such false promises as "How to lose ten pounds overnight" or "Quit smoking in one day." Some stores have the "biggest sale ever" once a month; it is amazing that their prices have not been reduced to zero after years of having the biggest sales. One foreign visitor wondered why American supermarkets do not have small eggs; the smallest are medium, and the sizes go up to large, extra large, and jumbo.

Another of the most abused words in America is *love*. Americans say "I love chocolate" or "I love spicy food." So *love* refers to something they are fond of. Since "I love you" is not enough, people add adverbs to emphasize the intensity of their love. In Asian families, couples rarely say "I love you" to each other, but their marriages last longer than do Americans'. Inflated words give outsiders the impression that Americans are insincere or naive.

Language defines a culture, its perceptions, and its concept of reality. In the United States, there is great respect for the power of hyperbole. In contrast, in Asia, exaggeration creates skepticism concerning the veracity of words. Asians do not trust overconfident people. A researcher interviewed both Asian and American children about how they thought they had done on a math test. The American children said that they had done well, whereas their Asian counterparts said that they had not done so well. In reality, the Asian children outdid the Americans. Whereas Americans indulge in overstatement, Asians are inclined toward understatement. Interestingly, the tendency to overestimate does not stop as one ages. In a recent study, psychologists found that incompetent adults overestimate their abilities, leading them to erroneous conclusions and unfortunate choices.

Certainly, false modesty is not a virtue either; however, it is important for people to assess themselves and their situations accurately. Although modesty is not an American strength, honoring the hierarchy of language will help Americans come across as more genuine and sincere.

Prejudice

Despite the growing appreciation for cultural diversity in America, racism and intolerance, though often subtle, are still in evidence. Americans represent every race and nearly every ethnic group in the world. People of different cultures live and work in the same place, sharing a community. All Americans fight together when America is at war; many ethnic groups, particularly Latinos and blacks, have already fought for the country in World War II, the Vietnam War, and the Gulf War. In peace, Americans collectively compete against other countries in the global economy. They cannot afford to lose their edge because of their ethnic diversity. Besides, there is increasing racial and ethnic mixing in the United States. In his book *Global Me*, G. Pascal Zachary observed that more Americans are developing flexible identities as the new multicultural American transcends the hyphenated identities of a generation ago. According to Zachary, new Americans live both within and beyond the traditional boundaries of ethnoracial identities, and their diversity is a big advantage for the nation's political and cultural power.

In fact, America's superpower status has been achieved through the contributions of various newcomers. In 1621, an officer of the Virginia Company dispatched a group of Italian glassblowers to Jamestown. Those Italian craftsmen were among the first immigrants to help build a new nation. Later, Irish stonemasons helped build U.S. canals, and Chinese laborers helped construct North America's transcontinental railroads. In the 1970s and 1980s, it was common to find East Indian engineers writing software programs in Silicon Valley. These days, visiting a high-tech company is like visiting a United Nations building. And many immigrants have led the signature American corporations. They include former CEO of Coca-Cola Roberto Goizueta, a Cuban immigrant; former CEO of Intel Andrew Grove, an immigrant from Hungary; CEO of Computer Associates, Charles B. Wang, an immigrant from China; and Jerry Yang, cofounder of Yahoo, an immigrant from Taiwan. They bring top technology, quality, and profitability to American businesses.

Unfortunately, despite the fact that more than thirty years have passed since the Civil Rights Act imposed a policy of racial neutrality, discrimination has not been eliminated in public or private institutions in the United States. According to a 1995 survey commissioned by the National Conference of Christians and Jews, 80 percent of African Americans, 60 percent of Latino Americans, and 57 percent of Asian Americans surveyed felt that their group did not have equal opportunities in the workplace. Many Americans who hold stereotypes about certain races refuse to give up their prejudices. While Americans often perceive racial matters as black or white issues, there are other minority groups who suffer from prejudices based on gender, religion, nationality, language, sexual orientation, accent, and so on. For example, many people thought that the bombing of the Oklahoma federal building was an act of terrorists from the Middle East before the real (American) suspects were identified. Although it seems like a harmless suspicion, it affected Americans of Middle Eastern heritage. One Arab engineer at a high-tech company said that he stopped going to the company cafeteria and ate his lunch at his desk because he sensed the hostility of other employees. The Iranian father of a teenager told me that he had to change her last name because she was harassed so much. It may be paranoia; it may not be.

Compared with many other countries, America's openness and hospitality toward people from different backgrounds are truly admirable. No Asian country has welcomed as many immigrants, nor have any European countries been as tolerant as the United States in accepting religious differences. Russians discriminate against Ukrainians and other minorities. Many Asians are notorious for their prejudice against outsiders, especially people of color. Foreigners in Japan call themselves "forever *gaijin*" because the Japanese rarely accept them. More than 750,000 Koreans face discrimination in Japan. Japan's National Police Agency has been uneasy about the estimated 300,000 illegal laborers in the country, and has issued memos about the problem, such as the one that warns that Pakistanis have "a unique body odor" and carry infectious diseases. The Japanese are not the only Asians who are discriminatory. The Chinese and Koreans are prejudiced against people with different backgrounds and even against people from certain regions of their own countries. Ethnic tension persists in Malaysia, Indonesia, and Thailand.

Although prejudice against groups different from one's own seems universal, valuing diversity is a must for Americans if they want their country to be a true leader in the world—economically, politically, and morally. They should strive for zero tolerance of any kind of racism; all groups should give up their animosity toward other groups. Victor Frankl, a survivor of Auschwitz, wrote, "There are two races of men in this world, but only these two—the 'race' of the decent man and the 'race' of the indecent man."

To create a nation of decent men and women, it is important to become aware of one's biases and prejudices and learn to get beyond them. Regardless of one's ethnicity, everyone has had the experience of being hurt by others' prejudices with regard to various factors, from physical size to intelligence. Even children say that they suffer from the prejudices of their classmates. Letitia Baldridge, in her book *More than Manners*, listed the reasons why a child feels victimized. They include being of a different race, color, nationality, or religion; being rich or poor; being too smart or not smart enough; being too pretty or too unattractive; being athletically challenged; and so on. Although she didn't list it, being an outstanding athlete also creates negative stereotypes among some groups. One thirteen-year-old football player said that he was stereotyped as being dumb. The problem is that not all adults outgrow their childish exclusion of people who are different. Many people have stereotypes about almost everyone who is different from themselves.

What America needs is to build a more inclusive culture, one that will fully utilize the contributions of all Americans who have diverse backgrounds and talents. As Anthony Appiah, a Harvard University professor who was born in Ghana, wrote, "The humanist requires us to put our differences aside; the cosmopolitan insists that sometimes it is the differences that make it rewarding to interact at all." The United States has already proved that diversity strengthens its global competitiveness. Now if Americans can live with diversity in harmony and unity, through creative and peaceful conflict resolution, they will be the true envy of the world.

Tolerance of Violence

When I travel around the world, I have a tendency to ask the locals about their perceptions of America. One view they all seem to share is their horror at the level of violence in the United States. Unfortunately, their perception matches reality. Violent crime in the U.S. has more than tripled since 1965. The U.S. homicide rate is 7 times that of Finland, 20 times that of Germany, and 40 times that of Japan. In most large U.S. cities, one is advised not to go out alone late at night. In certain areas of New York, Los Angeles, Chicago, Houston, and Detroit, one doesn't feel safe even during the daytime. Washington, D.C., the nation's capital, was once known as the murder capital, with one of the highest homicide rates in the country.

Every morning and evening, Americans are bombarded with the bad news: murders, rapes, gang violence, drug-related crimes, and so on. Out of fear, they spend billions of dollars to protect their lives and property, including burglar alarm systems in their houses, double locks, and lockable windows. Car owners have security systems installed. And Americans practice their right to bear arms. Many buy guns, keep guns at home, carry guns with them, and keep guns in their cars. Still, they do not feel safe. So they learn self-defense skills at martial arts schools. Today, Americans are more paranoid about their own safety and that of their families than they have ever been.

If Americans want to keep their country safe, why do they sell violence in the media? In the book *The China that Can Say No*, one coauthor described his physical reaction after he saw the movie *Natural Born Killers,* directed by

Oliver Stone. While he was watching the movie, his body was soaked with sweat. After the movie, his friend asked him, "Don't you feel like killing somebody, too?"

Why don't parents protect children from violent images on television, in video games, in movies? A study at the University of Illinois concluded that American children watch 200,000 violent images and 40,000 murders on television alone by the age of eighteen and that those who are exposed to violence tend to be more abusive of their spouses and children. If they are more abusive of their family members, wouldn't they be more violent toward friends and neighbors too? Even if some scholars argue that exposure to violent images doesn't necessarily increase violent behavior, such images are certainly not a positive influence on children. Interestingly, Asian children are also exposed to comic books and video games that are filled with violence or sex. Yet Asian nations don't experience the high rate of violent crime that America does.

In my opinion, if Americans want to reduce violent crimes, they must control guns. In all Asian countries, gun ownership is illegal for virtually all civilians. Asians don't understand why many Americans are obsessed with owning guns. The price for this right has been high. In 1996, handguns were used to murder 2 people in New Zealand, 1 in Japan, 30 in Great Britain, 106 in Canada, 213 in Germany, and 9,390 in the United States. With this disturbing statistic, those Americans who defend their constitutional right to bear arms must ask whether they are willing to see their families gunned down by others who hold the same belief.

Most countries that permit the possession of guns by civilians have much tougher laws than the United States does. In 1997, Britain passed a bill that outlaws all handguns—after a gunman had shot and killed some children and their teacher in 1996. In Germany, anyone wanting to own a handgun must first join a target-shooters club for a year of instruction. After confirming that the person is not dangerous, the shooting club applies to the local police, who then do a background check. In contrast, in the U.S., even children can order guns from mail-order companies or over the Internet. It is outrageous that many schools have had to start using metal detectors to screen incoming students for weapons. Even the very young are not immune to the violent images they are exposed to. At a day-care center, a four-year-old boy told me that he was in trouble because he had said that he was going to bring a gun and shoot everyone. When I asked why, he said that one of his classmates had been mean to him. I didn't believe that this sweet boy was really capable of doing so. However, it was scary to think that such a young child would even consider using a gun to resolve a conflict with a friend. How can we expect our children to be motivated to learn in an environment where they don't feel safe?

It costs over thirty thousand dollars a year to send a youth through a rehabilitation program, but even these programs are not very effective. Once teenagers have had a brush with the law, they often travel further down the road of crime. In fact, they can sharpen their "expertise" in prison, where they are surrounded by more experienced criminals. Thus, Americans should invest in crime prevention rather than correction.

Streets and schools are not the only places Americans worry about. Companies are also worried about increasing workplace violence, and many are taking measures to effectively handle disgruntled employees. Violent crimes can happen in many ways, but certainly guns make it easier to kill or wound, especially multiple victims.

If Americans want to keep their country safe, the punishment must fit the crime. In Asia, the penalties for crimes are much harsher than in the United States. In Singapore, drug trafficking is punishable by death. As one American teenager painfully discovered, defacing a car with spray paint brings the stiff penalty of cane lashes across one's back and a prison sentence. In most Asian countries, a person convicted of murder serves life in prison with no parole or gets the death penalty. In China, capital punishment is imposed not only for murder but also for other offenses, including rape and drug trafficking. Justice is swift and brutal. In contrast, the average sentence for murder in the U.S. is just under eighteen years, but the average murderer serves just over eight years of his or her sentence. Furthermore, a criminal case can linger in court for years. As a result, people perceive that the criminal justice system in America is in a state of collapse: there are formalities and technicalities but little common sense—and little justice.

According to Confucius, in societies where people are disciplined by laws rather than social convention, people break the law when it suits their purposes. Thus, it is all the more important to emphasize character education, along with controlling guns and violence in the media.

Contentiousness about Religion

At lunch, a potential client and I started talking about the cultures of the world. When the conversation shifted to our backgrounds, she shared her faith, which was Catholicism, with some Mexican folk practices thrown in. She talked about how her prayers had helped her get the job she wanted. She also told me how her father's cancer had been cured with his visualization of the cancer cells leaving his body. When we walked out of the restaurant, I thanked her for sharing her story about the power of faith. She said, "I was asking myself whether I could share with you or not. It's kind of risky these days to talk about such things. But my spirit told me it was okay."

When Asians learn English, they are told not to discuss sex, religion, or politics with Americans. I once heard it said that "in New York, if someone mentions God at a party, he'll be met with silence. If he mentions God a second time, he will never be invited back." It seems strange that in a country where freedom of speech and freedom of religion are guaranteed, people are afraid to talk about their faith for fear of offending somebody. The Pledge of Allegiance states, "one nation, under God, indivisible," and U.S. currency is stamped "In God We Trust." Yet it is no longer fashionable to acknowledge God in public. When I went to a wedding recently, the officiating clergywoman never used the word *God*, replacing it with *the Supreme Being*.

The United States has already banned prayer in public schools. The Supreme Court has declared it unconstitutional to teach children that the nation was founded under God. In the business world, some consider it politically incorrect to display religious symbols or objects in the office. For example, a corporate recruiter was told to remove religious items from her desk; her supervisor was concerned about offending job candidates. The problem is that God is disappearing from Americans' conversations, and people seem to be more ready to talk about their sex lives than their spiritual lives. When people avoid discussing their faith in public, they distance themselves from the teachings and practices of their religions. However, if Americans really believe in others' freedom of religion, their society should provide a safe environment for discussing it. Although worship is a personal matter, no one should be ridiculed or punished for talking about his or her faith.

Once I read a letter to the editor in a local paper. The author wrote that she was tired of hearing people refer to good values as "Christian values." She argued that even though she was not a Christian, she was a good human being, a good wife, and a good mother. She had a point, but a good human being does not have to be offended because someone considers good values to be Christian values. I agree that there are wonderful people who do not practice any religion or acknowledge any God at all. However, just as nonbelievers are free not to worship God, believers should be free to worship God or express their faith in their own way.

In Korea, I went to a high school whose founder was Christian. The students did not choose the school themselves; the selection was made by a government lottery system. The students were required to attend a weekly religious service, and no parents complained or asked that their children be exempted from that requirement. In

Thailand, where the official religion is Buddhism, affluent parents are eager to send their children to Catholic private schools, even if they practice Buddhism at home. Neither parents nor students complain that their rights are being violated. Parents believe that any religion is better than no religion, because it teaches their children to do good and be good. Parents may not want their children to convert, but they tend to agree with the saying of the Dalai Lama, the Tibetan Buddhist monk who won a Nobel Peace Prize: "Any religion that teaches love for humanity is worth believing in." Even in China, where religious freedom is more limited than in the United States, some factory owners encourage their workers to attend Christian worship services, justifying their leniency by saying, "These workers, if they listen to the word of God, won't steal from me. I tell them they should study the word of God and improve themselves."

In the United States, people are too easily offended by the slightest infringement on their religious or other rights. Some are even offended by Christmas trees in front of public buildings or Christmas cookies served at school. Although Christmas has become almost a secular, commercialized event for many Americans and non-Americans, increasing numbers of U.S. companies have renamed their traditional Christmas party a "holiday party," so as not to offend non-Christians. I admire their effort to be inclusive; however, real inclusiveness requires people to have tolerance for differences.

Despite their Christian foundation, Americans have been tolerant of other religions or "nonconventional" denominations for over two hundred years—as long as these believers didn't practice or proclaim their faiths openly.

However, if people of all faiths or no faith could practice acceptance of and tolerance for people who wish to practice their faith openly, America would be a more harmonious place.

I once read about a prayer center in India founded by the late Mother Teresa. It is a place for all who want to pray, regardless of their religion. So when Hindus come to pray, they pray that they will become better Hindus, and if Muslims walk in, they pray that they will become better Muslims.

Arrogance

Although many Americans do a lot of things right, they are criticized for being too judgmental about the values and practices of other countries. Americans' open criticism has caused world leaders to complain about U.S. arrogance. Former Soviet president Mikhail Gorbachev wrote, "If Americans think that the world will be happier with the adoption of the American lifestyle, it [this belief] is as dangerous as communism." From Kuala Lumpur to Tokyo, Asian values are gaining a new meaning for those who want to recover their cultural identity. As Tom Plate, a *Los Angeles Times* columnist, warned, "Our misplaced sense of cultural superiority riles up anti-Americanism throughout Asia, especially among student groups, the region's future leaders."

Although the United States has created a model for a democratic country, Americans cannot say how other countries should be governed. In the best-seller *The China that Can Say No*, a Chinese businessman and poet wrote about an incident between a former U.S. president and the late Deng

Xiao-Ping, who was premier of China at the time. The U.S. president expressed his concern about China's one-child-per-family policy and its impact on human rights. Deng listened carefully and responded, "We could accept your opinion; however, China can't afford to have an increase of 23 million people per year. So could you increase the quota of Chinese immigrants to the U.S. by 23 million per year? I believe your answer will be yes." Shocked by Deng's "request," the president suggested they change the topic.

Chinese Premier Li Peng had a point when he said, "For developing countries human rights are, first and foremost, the right to survive. A person must first survive before talking about rights." Within the inner cities of the United States, we see numerous examples of families and children trying to survive side by side with gangs and drug dealers. Yet neither China nor Japan tells the U.S. to remove all the guns from the streets. They do not tell Americans how to solve the problems of inner cities. Indians do not criticize Americans for consuming so much beef. Food is fundamental to a country's culture, rooted in its daily customs and traditions. A dish that may seem repugnant in one country may be a delicacy in another.

Most people in the world want to be respected for who they are. Some countries may not have accomplished as much as America has economically or technologically, but they may have long cultural heritages they are proud of, thousands of years of history and distinctive cultures. It seems that in the minds of some Americans, historical greatness and tradition are irrelevant, and the role of the rest of the world is to serve the United States and eventually learn from it. Asian leaders and followers call this attitude cultural imperialism. For many Asians who value history and tradition, America is a young country without a respectable culture.

If Americans want to earn the respect of Asians and persuade them to believe in "Americanism," they should stop judging situations from their own perspective. It is true that American democratic ideals have inspired other countries' opposition leaders to fight against dictatorship, but to deserve the respect and admiration of others, Americans must strive harder to be worthy of leading the world. A lot of American practices are not well regarded by other countries, even by some Americans. In August 1999, Thomas L. Friedman wrote in the *New York Times*, "The idea that the U.S. Congress, looking at a $1 trillion surplus, wants to cut its paltry foreign aid budget, refuses to pay its U.N. dues, talks about free trade but then won't even expand NAFTA to Chile, and treats foreign policy as a sport in which you pass sanctions against your favorite enemy, like a game of darts, should embarrass every American."

Americans should learn not to do unto others what they would not have done unto them. One case in point is the sale of tobacco. In 1964, the American government first realized that cigarettes were a major cause of disease and death; reportedly, each cigarette smoked takes an average of seven minutes off one's lifetime. As a result of a three-decade-long antismoking campaign, the United States now has one of its lowest smoking rates ever—25.5 percent of the population. Former vice president Al Gore made an emotional appeal about the dangers of cigarette smoking at the 1996 Democratic Convention. However, America sells cigarettes to Asia without any regard for the health of its citizens. While

American domestic cigarette consumption has decreased by 20 percent since 1975, cigarette shipments to overseas markets have soared by 340 percent. In addition, as a result of this decline in the U.S., cigarette makers have shifted their marketing focus, and although adult smoking has declined, teenage smoking has climbed. Of course, the U.S. is not the only one to blame. Some Asian governments have monopolies on tobacco sales and collect hefty import and sales taxes at the cost of their own citizens.

If America wants to be a moral leader, it should hold a higher standard for itself. The ancient Chinese character for business meant life with meaning. American business leaders should keep this in mind when they seek profits around the world.

When Americans feel self-righteous, they should ponder what the great anthropologist Edward T. Hall said: "Accept the fact that there are many roads to truth and that no culture has a corner on the path or is better equipped than others to search for it."

Part Three

Invitation to Global Virtues

Cultural understanding is a long journey. The more I see of the world and the more people I meet, the more I realize how little I know and how limited my perspective is. Beginning to understand Americans' national culture and its cultural strengths and weaknesses is only the beginning in the journey toward global citizenship. Despite the differences across cultures, however, there are common values that will help us form a more peaceful global village. In this part I list the ten global virtues that in my opinion will connect us.

Top Ten Global Virtues

1. Know Your Own Culture

2. Seek to Understand Others

3. Do Not Judge

4. Respect the Divine

5. Practice Kindness and Politeness

6. Remember Your Responsibilities

7. Honor Your Family

8. Invest in Human Relationships

9. Use Moderation

10. Learn and Teach

Know Your Own Culture

From Socrates to modern-day leadership gurus, wise men and women in history have encouraged self-knowledge as a source of wisdom and virtue. To develop ourselves, we must know our culture, including national, ethnic, and regional cultures. Each of us is a product of our cultural background, including gender, ethnicity, family, age, religion, profession, and other life experiences. Our cultural inventory provides us with valuable insights for understanding our beliefs and attitudes, our values and assumptions. Thus, it is critical that we reflect on the various aspects of our own cultural identity and examine their positive and negative impacts on our personal and professional development.

To a certain extent, our regional background determines what is appropriate and what is not. When we hear "I'm a country girl," "She is a Yankee," "He is from California," or "He is a typical midwesterner," we have a distinctive image of that person. One man who grew up in south Texas said that the hardest thing he had to do after he joined a high-tech firm in a big city was to eliminate "Yes, sir" and "No, sir" from his vocabulary. His boss told him it was unacceptable. One executive from Wisconsin said that in the 1980s, nobody in her town would have felt comfortable driving a foreign car because everyone had a family member working for an American automaker. It is important to find out whether we hold on to any special regional attitudes that can be barriers to our open-mindedness. Ideally, all Americans should aspire to travel to all fifty states to appreciate their country. Many Americans have culture shock when they move not to a foreign land but within their own country. Each state has distinctive characteristics and cultural rules, although there is a sense of commonality and predictability across America.

It is also important for all Americans to understand their ethnic heritage. On the scale of cultural difference, researchers point out that there are more cultural differences between white Americans and some ethnic Americans than there are between Americans and the British. Thus, those who strongly identify themselves as "hyphenated" Americans might want to learn about the impact of their unique cultural heritage on their values and behaviors.

Gender and age are two other important elements of culture. Especially in certain ethnic groups, distinctive role expectations are imposed on men and women. For classifying age groups, we have the silver generation, the Depression generation, baby boomers, X generation, Y generation, Net generation, and so on; all generations identify with unique events, experiences, music, and idioms that are meaningful only to them. Thus, we must understand our own generational values as they differ from other generations.

Our profession, work ethic, and habits are also important elements of culture. Our jobs and professions affect how we see the world, how we solve problems, how we interact with others, and what we have in common. Some may be surprised to learn that many professions share similarities across cultures. For example, any military person in the world knows about the commonality of the military culture—a strict hierarchy and a sense of duty. An engineer from Malaysia may have more in common with an American engineer than with a Malaysian lawyer.

Economic background is another important factor in understanding our values and assumptions. People who survived the Great Depression definitely have different attitudes toward money. Self-made people value work in ways that people who have inherited wealth do not. Some Americans, however, take all their comforts for granted and consider many of their luxuries to be necessities.

Finally, to know ourselves, we must understand our unique personal background and experience. The families we grew up in and the families we have now have a tremendous impact on our view of the world. While filling out a questionnaire about her family background, one manager shared that her tendency to micromanage was derived from her childhood. Her parents had divorced when she was only ten, and as the oldest child in the family, she had to take care of her younger siblings. To do that job well, she had to put her hands on everything that her little brothers and sisters did. More than twenty years later, she still feels that she has to do the same for her staff.

Every experience, positive and negative, contributes to our identity. So it is worthwhile to take an inventory of our background to discover who we are and to determine whom we want to become.

Seek to Understand Others

Understanding and accepting other cultures involves two distinct elements for Americans: one is understanding cultures in the United States that are different from one's own; the other is understanding the cultures of other nations. Differences can create misunderstanding, but positive resolution from creative tension makes interaction enriching and rewarding.

Once we recognize the impact of our culture on our own attitudes and behaviors, it is natural that we develop an interest in other cultures. Traveling overseas is a great way to experience other cultures. Although the United States is number one in some areas, there are virtues or practices to be learned from other cultures as well. Tom Peters, author of many best-sellers, wrote that the most outstanding customer service he had ever experienced was at a hotel in Bangkok. "Take a vacation to Bangkok, but write it off—in good conscience—as business travel. That's legit if you stay at the Oriental; just watching its staff perform is an advanced course in service quality," wrote Peters in his book *The Pursuit of WOW!* Many other people, including inventors, artists, and architects, have gotten brilliant ideas while away from home. For example, the Japanese engineer at Toyota who invented the JIT (just-in-time) manufacturing process got the idea at a U.S. grocery store. During his visit to the U.S., he was impressed with the efficient process of quickly restocking a product on the shelf after a sale, and wanted to find a way to apply the process to manufacturing a car. If we are observant, the whole world is a classroom. Traveling encourages us to live beyond our comfort zones. On the road, we are likely to meet people we would not normally associate with. Traveling challenges our preconceptions and assumptions about others and ourselves. Being in a foreign country also helps us discover new aspects of our identity. Novelist Richard Stern describes how he found a new personality in a new place: "I yearned to go abroad when I was young, reading Hemingway, Fitzgerald, and so on. And once I went there it was extremely exciting for me to become a new personality, to be detached from everything that bound me, noticing everything that was different."

For those who can't afford overseas travel, there are many other ways to improve one's understanding of other cultures. The Internet provides us with virtual international travel. Watching foreign movies or videos is another great way to appreciate different ways of living. Many cities have international hospitality committees and host intercultural events. Companies sponsor events that promote cultural understanding within their diverse workforce. Attending cultural events for groups other than our own helps us see the commonality among different groups.

Cultural curiosity enriches us all as we challenge our preconceptions about other countries and cultures. It is unfortunate that political correctness in the United States has caused people to avoid asking about other people's culture for fear of offending someone. Yet most people are more than willing to share their cultural background with someone who is ready to really listen. When we genuinely seek understanding of others, we can open and maintain a dialogue with people who have different looks, ideas, opinions, and so forth. We also need to practice listening to others. The Chinese symbol for listen contains the characters for ear, eye, and heart. We must listen to others with our ears, eyes, and heart and give them our undivided attention. Above all, we must be open-minded to the experiences of others. Many leaders are open-minded in that sense. Bill Gates, former CEO of Microsoft, is known for reading entire magazines in fields different from his main industry. His reasoning is that if he pursues only what he knows and likes to read, his mind will not expand. Personally, I am grateful to many of my friends and acquaintances in different fields for expanding my horizons. A publisher and editor friend taught me the value of a book. "A book is a universe. When a reader opens a book, she is taken to a new world she didn't know about before." A sushi chef taught me the importance of visualizing my goals. To make beautiful sushi, he always visualized the final form he wanted to create before he started. A banker friend taught me how to better achieve my goals by identifying my personal assets and liabilities.

Seeking to understand others also applies to our personal hobbies. Former CEO of Coca-Cola Doug Ivester argues, "If you hate the symphony, you should go to the symphony. If you hate country music, you should go to a country music concert." Indeed, many performers have converted me to types of music that I would not normally have listened to before I saw them in action. This is a good lesson about not making up our minds about something before we fully experience it.

Above all, when we seek to understand others, others will seek to understand us.

Do Not Judge

I learned one of the most important lessons of my U.S. graduate education in a political economy class taught by Dr. Ray Marshall, former secretary of labor under President Jimmy Carter. He asked us to study the pros and cons of numerous controversial policies in preparation for the next class. Then, during class, each of us had to flip a coin, and depending on how it landed, heads or tails, we had to take the pro or con side in a debate, regardless of our personal beliefs. Many of the students already had strong opinions about each issue; however, as a result of the debates, they learned to be more open-minded before taking a position and to be more tolerant after taking one.

"Thou shall not judge" has become the eleventh commandment for many Americans. They are proud of America's tradition of tolerance, which has allowed diversity of opinion. Now, Americans must learn to apply their tolerance of differences beyond U.S. borders. Once they start learning about other countries, their histories and cultures, they will find it more difficult to judge them. People judge others when they don't know them or when they fear them. In extreme cases, they dehumanize people who are different, regarding them as "the other." One foreign visitor said that it took him a few years to learn to withhold judgment about seemingly "strange American behaviors." He concluded that if he thought American behavior was strange, Americans would think his behavior was strange, too. Once he reached that conclusion, he became more open to appreciating cultural differences without judgment.

The best practice in dealing with other cultures is to accept cultural differences as natural. Then we will not demand that "our" ways be followed, and we will not be easily offended by "their" ways. In fact, the Bible teaches us not to judge anyone, even those from our own culture. Once we know the life story of another person, when we can understand their pain and sorrow, we will have more compassion. Henry Wadsworth Longfellow said, "If we could read the secret history of our enemies, we should find in each man's life sorrow and suffering enough to disarm hostility." Examining the background of another person also helps in family relationships. When I was at college, I resented my mother for many things. But one day I objectively reviewed her life experiences. She had lost her father as a teen and had to support her family. Throughout her life, all she knew was duty as a daughter, wife, and mother. She never did anything just for herself and would not even know how to do so. Once I saw her life from this perspective, I had so much compassion for her that I could feel nothing but love.

In his book *The Great Gatsby*, F. Scott Fitzgerald wrote, "Whenever you feel like criticizing anyone, just remember that all the people in this world haven't had the advantages that you have had." A thirteen-year-old boy with very limited physical abilities said in a poem, "Judging another is judging God." Definitely, no one is wise enough to judge God.

Respect the Divine

Kei-Ten-Ai-Jin ("Respect the divine and love people") is the motto for Kyocera, a Japanese corporation. In fact, many Asians believe and live that philosophy. Regardless of one's religious or spiritual status, respecting the divine is the basis of global virtue and wisdom, as it teaches us humility, integrity, honesty, compassion, and generosity. Only with respect for the divine can we achieve true humility, because we know that every achievement is a gift from God. We may play a part in creating our own luck, but only if we are humble can we acknowledge that we couldn't have succeeded without divine guidance. President Abraham Lincoln confessed that many nights he knelt down on his knees and prayed for divine guidance. Only with the help of the Supreme Power did he become one of the greatest presidents in U.S. history.

Respecting the divine helps us maintain our integrity. During the Han dynasty in China, there was a period of political chaos. The government was filled with corrupt bureaucrats and opportunists. However, a governor of one province was a man of integrity. One night, someone came and presented him with a pile of gold as a bribe. The visitor said, "Please accept this, since nobody knows." The governor scolded the man and said, "The Heaven knows, the Earth knows, I know, and you know. How could you say that nobody knows?" When we are aware of a higher power, we tend to be more honest because we know that we will eventually have to account for our actions.

When we respect the divine, we take our job seriously, however humble it may be. We give every task our best effort when we believe that our work is a calling from the divine. The Japanese have a saying, "The production of a grain of rice is as great as the creation of a mountain." The late Martin Luther King Jr. said that even a street sweeper can be truly great if he sweeps the streets with grace—if in his heart he is giving his all.

When we respect the divine, we do not worship money. Those who believe that money is given from the divine are more likely to share what they have. When we respect the divine, we not only value money less but also treat every living thing more gently and kindly, even those who have harmed us. We seek our purpose for being in this world and pursue something greater than ourselves. We live our lives with grace and gratitude.

When we respect the divine, we are granted the power to forgive ourselves and others. The world is full of people who cannot do either. They suffer from excruciating rage and pain. Only as we learn to accept what we cannot change will we have peace within. The Koran, the holy book for Muslims, teaches that God will not change the condition of people until they change what is in their hearts. To bring peace to the world, we need more peace within ourselves.

Practice Kindness and Politeness

Ubuntu, a Nguni word, refers to a concept or philosophy that all Africans know. Although it is not easily translatable, it basically means the quality of being human, which includes kindness, consideration, compassion, generosity, hospitality, warmth, openness, and personal dignity. It also includes the spirit of willing participation and unquestioning cooperation. Africans understand that even if one has much of the world's riches and holds power or authority, without ubuntu one will not amount to much.

The discipline of developing a good heart is taught in many cultures and religions. The Dalai Lama said, "The proper utilization of our intelligence and knowledge is to effect changes from within to develop a good heart." Confucius taught that if you are generous, you will win many hearts; your good heart will touch others like flowers. Mother Theresa once took some rice to a hungry Hindu family. The mother of the family took half the rice and disappeared. When she returned, Mother Theresa asked where she had been. The mother answered that the family next door was hungry too. Considering that this neighboring family was Muslim, the Hindu mother was the model of ubuntu. When we practice ubuntu, we will be blessed with many new friends. The Arabs used to say that when a stranger appears at your door, feed him for three days before asking who he is, where he has come from, and where he is headed. That way, he will have strength enough to answer, or by then, you will be such good friends you won't care.

Although it's not always easy to be generous, it is important to remember humanity in every situation. John Kotter, a professor at Harvard Business School, wrote a book on the late Konosuke Matsushita, one of the most highly respected businessmen in Japan. He was the founder of Matsushita Corporation, including Panasonic. One day he went to a restaurant with other top executives and ordered a beef dish. When he had finished only half of it, he asked the restaurant manager to allow him to talk to the chef. The chef nervously came out from the kitchen, wondering what he had done wrong. Mr. Matsushita told the chef, "I just wanted to let you know that now that I am old, I cannot finish the full portion you have wonderfully prepared for me. I didn't want you to feel bad about the fact that I didn't finish the whole thing. There is nothing wrong with your cooking. I'm just too old to eat that much."

George Bernard Shaw said, "There is nothing easier than politeness, none more profitable." One of the problems of our modern, hectic lifestyle is that everybody is rushed and impatient, and civility is forgotten. More and more managers are concerned about their workplace protocol, and human resources departments are bringing in etiquette experts to help their employees practice civility. "Road rage" and even "air rage" are escalating at an alarming rate. Yet the most important element of courtesy is not good manners but good hearts. In a society or at a workplace, we may be able to impose civility and good manners, but we cannot bring about a change of heart, nor can we demand tolerance or acceptance by enforcing rules and regulations.

Thus, we all need to practice ubuntu, not just with the people we like but also with the tailgater behind us or the telemarketer who calls during dinner. Even when we have a billing dispute with a customer service representative, it is important to remember that the person is only doing his or her job to make a living.

Asians believe that each person releases some kind of energy, or *ki*. Some ki promotes harmony; some, conflict. If one is kind and releases harmonious ki, the good spirit will circulate and enhance our lives. Ki transfer does not occur just among people; it also takes place between people and animals and even between people and plants. Many Asians say that cows shed tears when they are chosen to be sent to the slaughterhouse. They sense their imminent death at the hands of their owners. Some Asians are also convinced that if a caregiver keeps touching a leaf or talking to a plant, the leaf will be greener and the plant healthier.

According to Buddha, there are seven kinds of offerings that can be practiced by anyone. The first is the physical offering—the service of one's labor. The second is the spiritual offering—a compassionate heart toward others. The third is the offering of eyes—a warm glance at others, which will give them tranquility. The fourth is the offering of countenance—a soft look with a smile for others. The fifth is the oral offering—kind and warm words to others. The sixth is the seat offering—giving up one's seat to others. The seventh is the offering of shelter—letting others spend the night in one's home. When we demonstrate these offerings to others, society will be kinder and gentler.

Remember Your Responsibilities

During my freshman year at Seoul National University in Korea, I took an English literature class. Although I do not remember any of the literature I read for the class, I have never forgotten a lesson I learned from the instructor, Professor Kook. One day she said,

> What a privilege it is for you to attend a college, in fact the best university in Korea. You may think that you got here because you were the smartest in your high school. But while you enjoy the privilege, you have to think about all the people who make it possible for you to be in this class. The bus drivers who drive you here [very few college students in Korea had a car then], the janitors who open the school gates, the cleaners who clean this classroom, the garbage collectors who collect trash across campus, and so on.

She listed all the people that most of us never considered relevant to our college lives and often didn't even see as they went about their jobs. She went on, "You owe them something big for allowing you to enjoy your lifestyle. With your education, you should strive to improve the world to make their work worthwhile. Thus, your foremost important duty as a student is to study hard so that their work will not be wasted." Since then, I have tried to show my gratitude to the many men and women who faithfully do their jobs and, in so doing, enhance my comfort and convenience.

Everyone has obligations toward others. Employers have responsibility for their employees. During the IMF crisis in 1998, a founder and CEO of a major dairy product company in Korea had to file for bankruptcy. He gathered all his employees in the company auditorium and read his farewell message: "I am a sinner. With a repentant heart, I leave every possession of mine with the company, and I resign." He did exactly that. At age seventy-two, he had nothing left for himself. He felt personally responsible for the employees who would not have jobs because his company had failed. In a culture where an owner often prospers even when his company goes bankrupt, this CEO's example has won many hearts.

Workers have obligations to their employers, too. An engineering director of a company said about his workers, "In my generation, we thought that we owed good work to our company. These days, most of my young people think that the company owes them something." Because the U.S. job market has been strong for the last decade, American workers have enjoyed—and come to expect—unprecedented privileges and benefits, including stock options, flextime, generous bonuses, increased maternity (and in some cases paternity) leave, and so on. It is important, though, not to take one's job for granted or to forget one's responsibility to employers, customers, and other stakeholders.

Our responsibilities as citizens go beyond observing laws, rules, and regulations. In every area of life and in every role we play, we can have an impact on society. Whether our role is as a parent, teacher, student, sibling, friend, or member of a community, we can either improve or diminish the external and internal conditions for ourselves and others. As Frank Lloyd Wright said, "Life is only worth living if you can make it more beautiful than you found it."

Honor Your Family

Chinese philosopher Mencius said, "There are three joys of a gentleman—the first, to have both parents alive and brothers and sisters without any suffering; the second, not to have anything to be ashamed of before the Universe and other people; and the third, to educate talent." He did not include becoming rich or famous among the three joys, and he regarded family health and well-being as the highest priority.

If everyone strives to honor his or her family and create a loving, supportive environment, many of the social ills in America will disappear. Traditionally, in China, to honor his family a young man had to pass a difficult government exam and then enter public service. Becoming a mandarin and returning to his hometown in gilded clothes was a traditional sign of success. As the society becomes more diverse and young people pursue careers to their liking, they still have a desire to honor their families.

One important aspect of honoring the family is to keep the family's name untainted, that is, not to do anything dishonorable that would bring shame to the family. For husbands and wives, this means that they avoid causing their spouses grief or pain. For parents, it means not engaging in any activities that would bring shame or sorrow to their children. As an Asian saying goes, "Tigers leave their skin (leather) and men leave their name after they die."

To keep honor in our families, we need to teach our children discipline. As more people are enjoying unprecedented economic growth, many families find it difficult to teach the middle-class values of hard work, thrift, and moderation. However, one thing is certain: money cannot raise our children for us. Sometimes it is easy for parents to bribe children with toys and gifts or use the television or video games as a baby-sitter, but as Oprah Winfrey said, indulging children can be another form of abuse. In Spanish, there is a saying, "You never forget what you learned in the cradle." Asians also say that a habit formed at the age of three will last until the age of eighty. Thus, we need to help our children form good habits from an early age.

The best way to teach our children to honor the family is by showing them that we care. Recently, my sister and I discussed what we remember about our father. He didn't have the means to take us to fancy places or to buy expensive toys. In fact, he couldn't even buy all the books he wanted us to read. The country itself was poor then, and there were no school or public libraries where we could borrow books, so my father went to a used-book store nearby and persuaded the owner to loan books to his children. During summer vacations, we checked out two books a day and returned them the next day. Of course, we had to read all of them and write book reports. Anyway, my sister's memory was of the rice bowl he placed under a blanket to keep warm for her meal. When we grew up in Korea in the

1970s, we had no microwave oven or even a rice cooker to reheat rice or keep it warm. Often my sister came home late from after-school programs, but she knew that her rice would be warm because Father put her rice bowl on the heated floor (Korean heating system) under a blanket. One of my favorite memories of my father was him waiting for me in the rain at a bus station with an umbrella in his hand because I hadn't prepared for a change in the weather. It was interesting that we remembered only kind things he had done for us. Thanks to his example, we are determined to honor him by passing on his legacy to our children.

Despite all my professional and personal ambitions, my only earnest wish is this: someday I want my son to be able to say, "I had a very special childhood. My parents were very decent people and we had lots of fun."

Invest in Human Relationships

"It took one person to bring you into the world, but it will take six to take you back to the grave," says a French proverb. This reminds us of our dependence on others. As we consider life and death, we have to ask whether we will have not only those six—the people who will carry the casket—but also those who want to be there because we were special to them. We become fully human through other people, but the culture of individualism and efficiency discourages the building of close relationships with others. We are either too self-sufficient, too busy, or too proud to admit our need for others. Many Americans are desperate to have meaningful relationships and to feel that they belong, but they are, according to the title of a book on lonely

Americans, "Bowling Alone." Americans will have even more difficulty building relationships unless they make it a top priority.

To develop relationships, we should start with our families and take the time to get to know them. There is no need to debate quality versus quantity time to justify our work away from our families. If we know where our heart is, we know how to follow it. And being busy with jobs and other responsibilities is no excuse. Often my son calls me when I am preoccupied with something else. Sometimes I feel like saying, "Mom is busy," but then I imagine how I will feel when I get old and need him, and he says, "Mom, I'm busy."

Although it may not be efficient or convenient, families must take the time to *be* together, not just do things together. Unless people see one another or talk regularly, it's hard to develop bonds. Without any emotional attachment or commitment, a relationship can only be superficial.

We also need to take time to be a friend to others. Anna Lindsay wrote, "It costs to be a friend or to have a friend. There is nothing except motherhood that costs so much." It costs time, effort, love, patience, and understanding, but friends are one of the sweetest gifts of life; they can guide, support, and correct us in times of need. In choosing our friends, we would be wise to consider including people from different cultures, ages, educational backgrounds, professions, religions, ethnicity, and so on. If we spend time only with those similar to ourselves, our growth will be limited. As Richard Evan said, "A diversity of friendships is one of life's real enrichments. To learn of the goodness of those who are unlike us—their worth, their sincerity, their good hearts, their good minds, their good company—is rich and rewarding."

At work, it is important to spend time getting to know our partners, peers, and subordinates as people, not just as "head counts." One ex-Microsoft manager said that the culture of corporate America is sincerely insincere. But there is a heavy price to pay for being so efficient and superficial. In California, there is a consultant known as Dr. Jean. According to *Business Week*, companies send their technically superior but arrogant executives to her to hone their people skills. On their first visit, Dr. Jean gives her clients a checklist to assess their management style, and one of the questions on the list is, "Would your subordinate be happy to get stuck in an elevator with you?" Nobody is happy being stuck in an elevator, but her point is whether people feel comfortable around you.

Former British Petroleum chairman and CEO David Simon was once asked how he would like to be remembered. He answered, "I think one of the nicest epitaphs I've heard for anybody is: 'That's a guy I'd like to go and have a drink with.'" Even if we work in a fast-paced, demanding environment, we should be personable enough for others to get to know us. In fact, companies have found that when employees have a strong relationship with their boss or co-workers, they tend to stay with the company. Strong relationships are a must for effective global teamwork. Successful global teams have both high task orientation and high relationship orientation.

In our communities, we need to get to know our neighbors. Since Americans move an average of twelve or thirteen times during a lifetime—double the French or British number—it is not always easy to develop meaningful relationships with neighbors. However, according to child advocate Peter Benson, for children to develop positively, they should know at least six nonrelated adults across generations. Each of us could be one of those six people to the neighborhood children or to our sons' and daughters' school friends.

Bonaro Overstreet said, "We grow as our relationships grow. Where my relationships to others are soundly growing, I am growing. Where they are halted in their growth, I am halted. Where they are twisted in their growth, I am twisted in mine." Therefore, let's set aside our self-help workbooks and time management tools to simplify our daily tasks or track our time. Let us use our time to fully appreciate another human being.

Use Moderation

"Eat not to dullness. Drink not to elevation." The Thirteen Virtues of Benjamin Franklin start with the virtue of temperance. Three of his other virtues also require discipline and are related to temperance: self-control, frugality, and moderation. Franklin's virtues ring as true today as they did when he wrote them, but they are probably more difficult to achieve.

We can use moderation in our desire for material things. We must ask whether our self-indulgence and spending sprees add any value to our peace and happiness. Once, a rich woman in India visited the late Mother Teresa and asked what she could do to help the poor. Observing her wearing an expensive sari, Mother said, "You can start buying less expensive saris and give the difference to the poor." Some rich Americans live in unpretentious homes and maintain modest lifestyles, but Juliet B. Schor, author of *The Overspent American,* states that most of us could reduce our spending by 20 percent without feeling a sense of deprivation.

We can exercise moderation in our work. Certainly hard work is a virtue, but overwork is not. During his presidency, Ronald Reagan was often criticized for taking an afternoon nap. Upon hearing that, he quipped, "Certainly I haven't heard about anyone who died of hard work, but why take the risk?" Not long ago, I was watching a television program that focused on how people in various cultures perceive time differently. When the narrator asked, "Why do we spend so much time working while there are so many other enjoyable life experiences?" I had to think hard for an answer. Obviously, America's leadership is due in part to hard work, but is there too much emphasis on work? Are Americans obsessed with achievement and success to the detriment of all else? When a person is overworked and stressed, he or she is more irritable and confrontational. In a relationship, tired people are more prone to argument and have less tolerance for differences. This is helpful to no one—co-workers, friends, or family.

Moderation in pursuing hobbies, toys, and fun, including exercise or sports, is also important. Although two-thirds of Americans exercise too little, some people pursue exercise or sports to the detriment of their relationships with family and friends. In pursuing entertainment, we also need moderation. If we are continually immersed in the Internet, video games, radio, and television instead of spending time to quiet our minds and listen to our inner voices, we will lose ourselves in the process.

Asians believed that one of the greatest virtues was the avoidance of extremes, even the good and the fun. Once I found a Japanese cup with ten principles for a healthy mind and body.

> Less meat, more vegetables
> Less salt, more vinegar
> Less sugar, more fruit
> Less eating, more chewing
> Less clothing, more bathing
> Less talk, more action
> Less wanting, more giving
> Less worry, more sleep
> Less riding, more walking
> Less anger, more smiles

If we can practice Franklin's virtues with these principles, we will achieve more balance and peace in life. Moderation is simply living our lives more intentionally for the benefit of our minds, bodies, and souls.

Learn and Teach

Life is a continuous journey of learning, especially in our global village. There are many countries to visit and many cultures to experience. There is great art and literature to see or read. There are fascinating and wonderful people to meet. As our national and regional cultures come into close contact, they begin to change. Our only option if we are to be present in our global village is to be open-minded to learning; we must make every day a day for learning.

The best lifelong learners are often humble. Once I had an opportunity to consult the president of a large U.S. company on Asian business cultures. His resumé was very impressive. With a Harvard MBA, he had rapidly risen to the top. Since he already had extensive international experience, I asked him where he wanted to start his session. He answered, "Teach me as if I knew nothing." Then I realized how he had become so successful: his humbleness. As we learn about the world and others, we need to share our knowledge and experience with others. We must practice the philosophy "each one, teach one." Many cultures have emphasized the passing down of distilled wisdom throughout history. In Asia, it is common for elders to scold young boys or girls for their misbehavior even if they are complete strangers. Elders believe that they have an obligation to teach the next generation, since they have earned the wisdom. Buddhists also teach us that we fulfill our own destiny by teaching others lessons they must learn.

When there is so much misunderstanding across cultures, everyone has the opportunity to present his or her culture and enhance mutual understanding. Everyone can be an architect and repairer of cultural bridges within and without the United States. Even when we are faced with prejudices, we can learn to manage our anger and get over it with courage and grace.

An African American executive shared with me her story of overcoming prejudice. Not long after the Los Angeles riots, she was invited to speak at an executive education program at a California university. Her audience was a group of Asian government bureaucrats. When she took the podium, she sensed that the audience didn't respect her as a speaker. She guessed that being a woman and being black were two counts against her. Instead of feeling insulted or angered by the audience's response, she asked three questions:

1. How many of you think that I'm a single mother on food stamps?
2. How many of you think that I'm a drug addict or an alcoholic?
3. How many of you think that I was personally involved in the Los Angeles riots?

When the audience was silent, she moved on to her topic, and everyone listened. She had earned their respect by challenging their stereotypes of black women.

Throughout history, great leaders have been great students and teachers. If we are open and mindful, every day presents us with countless learning and teaching opportunities. There is a Chinese saying that when I am walking in a company of three, one of the others will certainly have something to teach me. So everyone learns, everyone teaches.

Lao Tzu said:

> Human beings are born soft and flexible;
> when they die they are hard and stiff.
>
> Plants arise soft and delicate; when they die
> they are withered and dry.
>
> Thus, the hard and stiff are disciples of
> death; the soft and flexible are disciples of
> life.
>
> Thus an inflexible army is not victorious,
> an unbending tree will break.

The stiff and big will be lowered; the soft
and flexible will rise.

If we are open and flexible to new experiences and are
willing to share what we learn from them kindly and gently,
we will enlighten ourselves and others day by day. As
Thomas Carlyle put it, "Let each become all that he was
created capable of being; expand, if possible, to his full
growth, and show himself at length in his own shape and
stature."

Endnotes

1. Alan Murray, "The American Century: Is It Going or Coming?" *The Wall Street Journal*, 27 December 1999.

2. John Caline, "What's Wrong with America: Open Season on Uncle Sam," *The Independent* of London, 10 May 1998.

3. Michael A. Ledeen, *Tocqueville on American Character* (New York: St. Martin's Press, 2000), 130.

4. Andrew Ferguson, "Inside the Crazy Culture of Kids Sports," *Time*, 12 July 1999, 60.

5. Kenzaburo Oe, *A Healing Family* (New York: Kodansha International, 1996), 52.

6. Bukkyo Dendo Kyokai, *The Teachings of Buddha* (Tokyo: Kosaido Printing House, 1966), 74.

7. Lin Yutang, "The Importance of Living," in *Profile of America*, comp. Emily Davie (New York: Thomas Y. Crowell, 1954), 393.